THE Celestial MESSAGE

Mike and Family,

You have enriched our lives, thank you!

[signature]

Copyright © 2013 by TGS International, a wholly owned subsidiary of Christian Aid Ministries, Berlin, Ohio. All rights reserved. No part of this book may be used, reproduced, or stored in any retrieval system, in any form or by any means, electronic or mechanical, without written permission from the publisher except for brief quotations embodied in critical articles and reviews.

For more information about Christian Aid Ministries, see page 177.

ISBN: 978-1-939084-37-8
Printed in China
Second Printing: July 2016

Published by:
TGS International
P.O. Box 355
Berlin, Ohio 44610 USA
Phone: 330-893-4828
Fax: 330-893-2305
www.tgsinternational.com
TGS0001258

Editors: Daniel Miller, Susan Oatney
Layout: Teresa Sommers
Cover Image: Mystic Mountain. Credits: NASA, ESA, and M. Livio and the Hubble 20th Anniversary Team (STScI).

It is my privilege to dedicate this book

to my Father in heaven.

It is He who has said, *I will receive you, and will be a Father unto you, and ye shall be my sons and daughters.* (2 Corinthians 6:17b, 18a)

And also to my wonderful wife,

Elizabeth Yoder, who passionately shares in all my joys and sorrows and is my real-life example of the love of our Father in heaven.

Also to my father (in loving memory) and mother,

Allen and Emma Yoder, for their dedication in teaching me the way of truth.

Contents

INTRODUCTION	VII
CHAPTER ONE **THE MESSAGE GIVER**	10
CHAPTER TWO **THE MESSAGE BEARERS**	20
CHAPTER THREE **PARADING PLANETS**	52
CHAPTER FOUR **GALAXIES: ISLAND UNIVERSES**	72
CHAPTER FIVE **NEBULAE: VEILS OF GLORY**	92
CHAPTER SIX **THE VIEW**	132
CHAPTER SEVEN **LIGHT AND CREATION**	138
CHAPTER EIGHT **THE MESSAGE**	150
GLOSSARY	166
IMAGE CREDITS	168

Introduction

Stretching all around us, across distances greater than the human imagination itself, are God's created heavens. Each particular speck of light we see bears witness of something far greater. From our perspective we see little more than flickering candles, weakly shimmering as if in the last moments of a fragile existence. But along with our growing understanding of what they are, we have also discovered why they appear so frail. It is simply because of their extreme distance from us.

For our own safety, these uncontrollable colossal giants of raging, roiling **plasma**[a] are positioned trillions of miles away. We are situated just close enough for comfort to the nearest one of them, our sun. But even at this distance of almost 93 million miles, we shudder to think what would happen should we be nudged just 5 percent closer. Venus, the next closest **planet** to the sun, is only about 25 percent closer to the sun than we are. The average temperature there, however, is over 860 degrees Fahrenheit, an intense heat which is a result of both its proximity to the sun and its thick blanket of sulfurous clouds.

These superpowers in space are also incredibly large. We could circle the sun once a day if we traveled at the previously unattained speed of 113,000 miles per hour. But, if we traveled at the same speed around the nearby star Betelgeuse, it would take over one and a half years to circle it. This, of course, will never be done because just to get to the star by traveling at the same speed would take 3.8 million years. Yet comparing even this distance to the grand scale of the **cosmos** is like focusing on a single step of a marathon.

In our **galaxy**, the **Milky Way**, there are approximately 100 billion stars. But the Milky Way is reduced to an insignificant ember when viewed in light of the sea of galaxies across the far reaches of space. For every one of the stars in our galaxy, we could find another entire galaxy of millions and billions of stars, with many of the stars possibly having planets in orbit around them. Across each galaxy God stretched a spectacular array of dramatic clouds of gas and dust called **nebulae**, which can extend trillions of miles through space. Scattered through this incredible spread of creativity are comets and asteroids, as well as strangely behaving and powerful **quasars**, **pulsars**, and **supernovas**.

We could ask: why the enormous size, why the dramatic display of power, and why the innumerable bodies in the heavens? The Creator has a purpose for everything He sets out to do. What is He showing us through the wonders of space? What is the message of the heavens?

---

[a] Words defined in the glossary (p. 166) are indicated in bold type the first time they are used.

EARTH

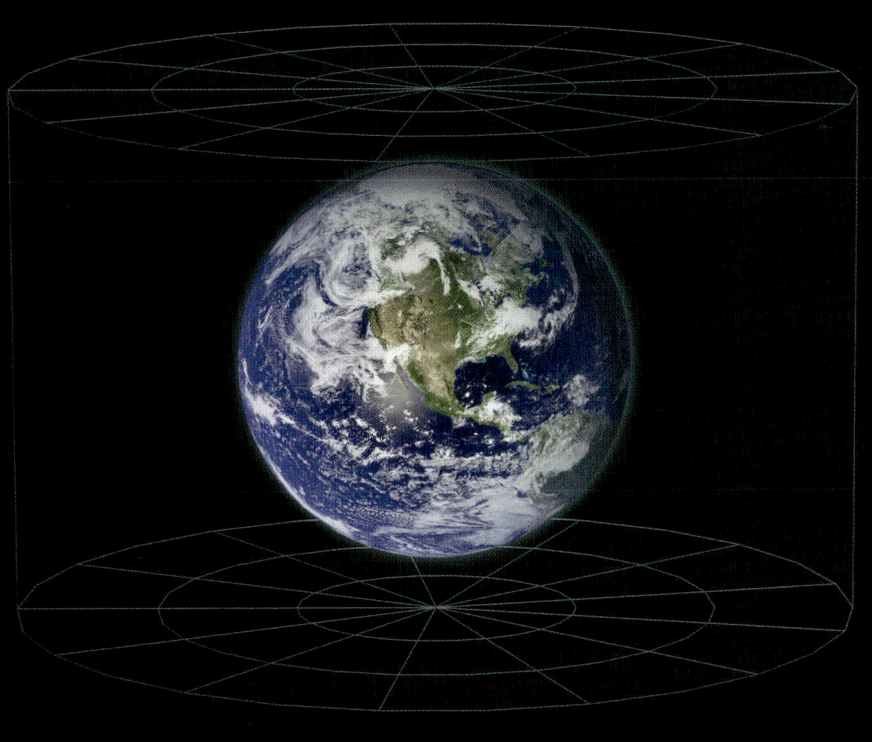

SOLAR SYSTEM

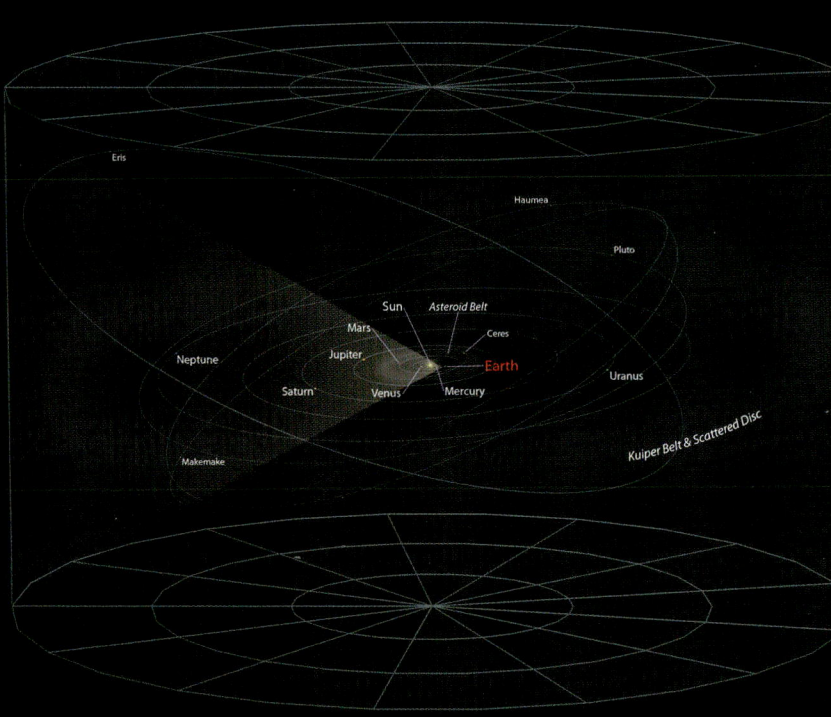

OBSERVABLE UNIVERSE

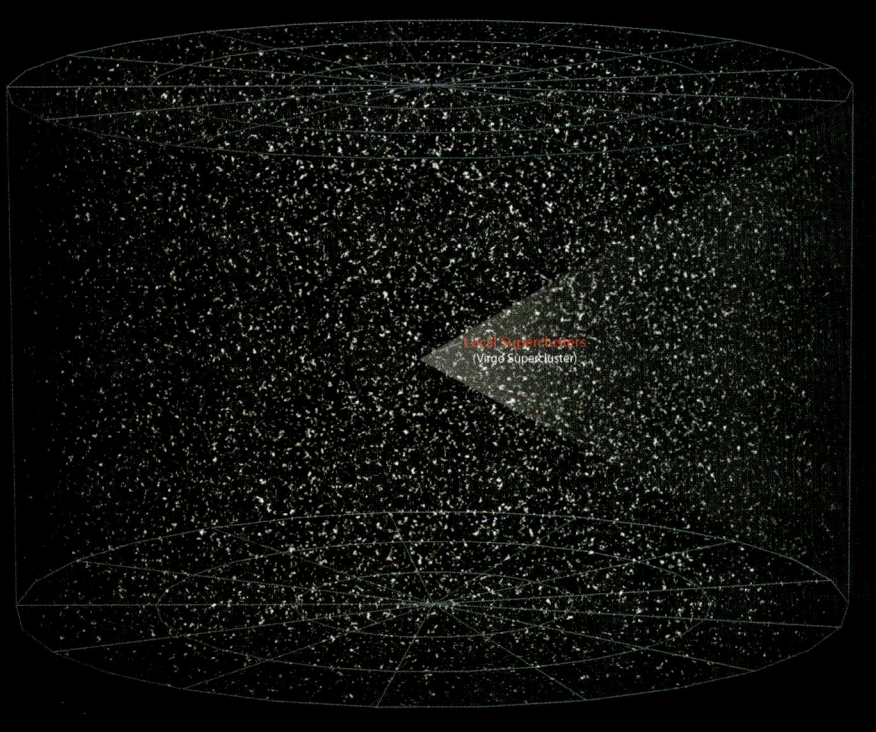

LOCAL SUPERCLUSTERS

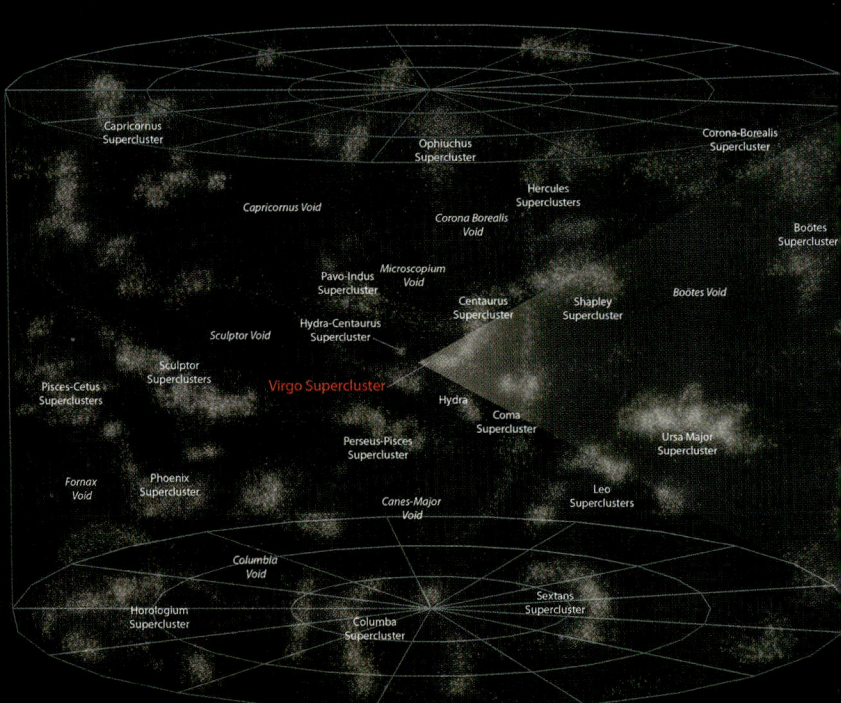

NEIGHBORING STARS

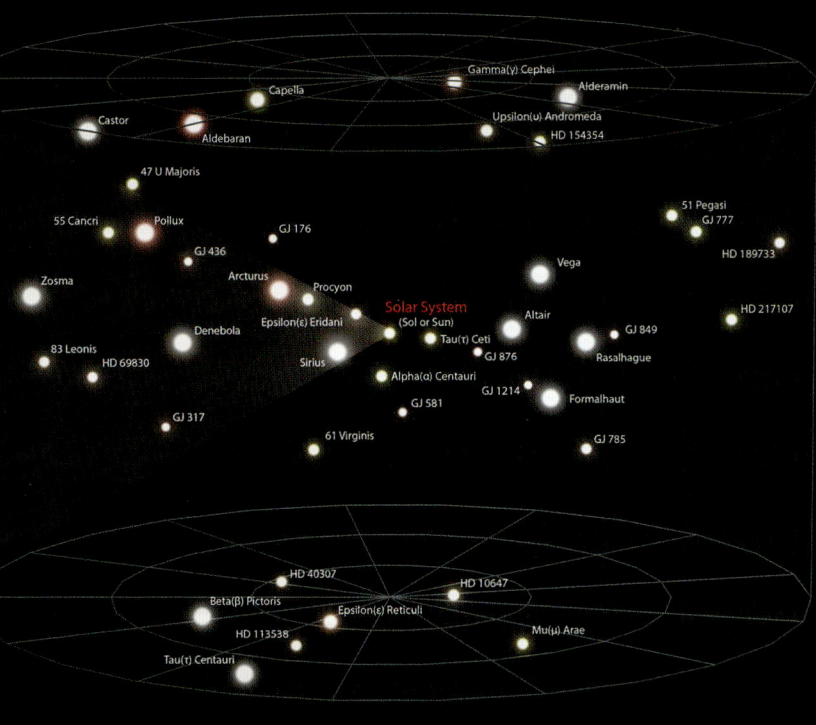

MILKY WAY

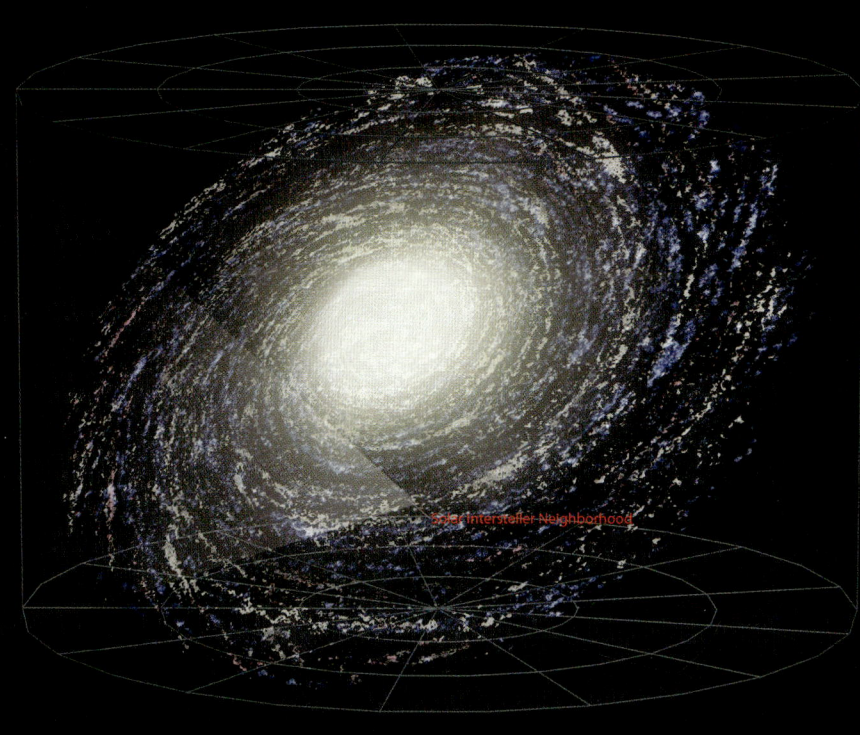

VIRGO SUPERCLUSTER

LOCAL GALACTIC GROUP

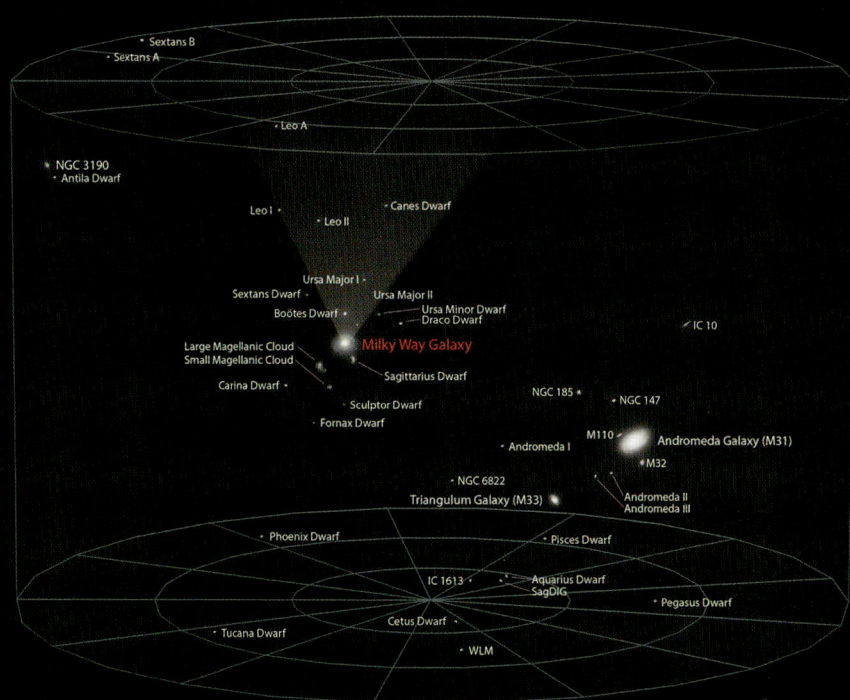

In the beginning God
CREATED THE HEAVEN AND THE EARTH.

The Orion Nebula shines in all its glory in this image taken at infrared wavelengths.

chapter one
The Message Giver

The Creator God is without compare. With mere words we cannot do justice to the reality of His nature. Neither can we fully comprehend the flitting rays of His glory that we see through our dim earthly vision.

His omnipotence is inexhaustible, His omniscience is infinite, and His omnipresence is boundless. His love, grace, and mercy are vast. His righteousness, justice, and holiness are perfect and beyond measure.

So when this great and infinitely powerful Jehovah God moves into action in the creation of a universe, the results are beyond measure. When the extensive repertoire of God's extraordinary ability is applied to a mission such as this, our weak minds wilt in trying to comprehend it. This mind-blowing creative act was not extraordinary for God; He was simply acting according to His character.

The God who can speak a universe into existence is an exciting God to learn about and serve. In His world, He has left His fingerprints. The grandeur of the universe offers an excellent opportunity to discover more of our Creator. In fact, according to the Bible, the heavens are the one part of the creation that explicitly declares the glory of God (Psalm 19). Night after night this giant billboard lights up, effortlessly advertising and proclaiming the wonder of the Creator. This proclamation is extended to the entire world, communicating without language barriers, as "there is no speech nor language where their [the celestial bodies'] voice is not heard." Indeed, the silent message can be deafening at times when its overwhelming reality sinks in.

Although the universe is one of the best showcases of the wonderful attributes of God, it is still inadequate for the task. Psalm 8:1 says of God, "O LORD our Lord, how excellent is thy name in all the earth! who hast set thy glory above the heavens." As strongly as God's glory is reflected in the universe, His true nature is far superior to anything He has made.

The universe is so large that we could never fully comprehend its size regardless of how long we apply our minds to the task. Proxima Centauri, the nearest star to us after our sun, is close to 25 trillion miles away. If we were to fly to this star at 25,000 miles per hour, the highest speed that man has ever traveled in a spaceship, it would take around 115,000 years before we'd arrive! Other stars in our own galaxy, the Milky Way, are nearly 15,000 times farther away than Proxima Centauri. And the Milky Way is only one of billions of galaxies scattered through the universe. The distance to the next closest one, the Andromeda Galaxy, is 500,000 times farther than the distance to Proxima Centauri.

As if these distances aren't big enough, the universe is getting even larger. How do we know this? First, God reveals it to us through His Word. The Bible mentions the expansion of the universe more than ten times.[a] Isaiah 40:22 says, "It is he . . . that stretcheth out the heavens as a curtain, and spreadeth them out as a tent to dwell in." Modern science now testifies to this as well. Astronomers discovered the expansion of the universe through natural means less than 100 years ago.

Men also assumed that the stars could easily be numbered. Tycho Brahe counted 777 stars. Johannes Kepler cataloged 1,005, and Ptolemy counted 1,056 stars. But the Bible plainly states that the stars are innumerable. "The host of heaven cannot be numbered . . ." (Jeremiah 33:22a). Today we know the number of stars is so large that we cannot hope to count them all. Astronomers have not even been able to successfully count the number of galaxies, and each one of them holds billions of stars. However, we can look at the stars we see around us and then extrapolate the approximate amount of stars in the observable universe. Using this method, astronomers have estimated 300 sextillion stars, a completely useless number for anyone other than a mathematician.

The Bible compares the number of stars in the sky to the number of sand grains on the seashore. Modern science also suggests that these two are nearly equal in number.[1] Visualize the sand of all the beaches around the world being stretched out into a single extensive shoreline. The sun would be equal to only one grain of sand among the untold trillions. The earth, which is one million times smaller than the sun in volume, would be equivalent to something smaller than a dust mite on the speck of sand. And, if every one of the seven billion people on the earth were to come together and stand in one place, with each one occupying three square feet, they would fit into a square less than 30 miles long on each side on this comparatively giant planet of 197 million square miles. So if the planet is a dust mite, this mass of people is just a whisker of peach fuzz on the mite's face. Where then does that leave me as one single, insignificant person? I'm like a strand of DNA dangling from the microscopic hair. This leaves us with nothing to say about ourselves and our accomplishments. Yet in spite of our smallness, *God* has something to say about us: we are the apple of His eye! The Creator even invested His life in ours for a reason that we cannot fully understand.

The Scriptures say that the earth is round. "It is he that sitteth upon the circle of the earth" (Isaiah 40:22). Men of ancient times, even long after Isaiah wrote this, believed the earth was flat. They also assumed the earth was supported by some physical means such as a giant human named Atlas or by enormous mythological creatures.[2] But believers in God have known for thousands of

---

[a] Job 26:7 He stretcheth out the north over the empty place, and hangeth the earth upon nothing.

Isaiah 40:22 It is he that sitteth upon the circle of the earth, and the inhabitants thereof are as grasshoppers; that stretcheth out the heavens as a curtain, and spreadeth them out as a tent to dwell in.

Isaiah 44:24 Thus saith the LORD, thy redeemer, and he that formed thee from the womb, I am the LORD that maketh all things; that stretcheth forth the heavens alone; that spreadeth abroad the earth by myself.

Zechariah 12:1 The burden of the word of the LORD for Israel, saith the LORD, which stretcheth forth the heavens, and layeth the foundation of the earth, and formeth the spirit of man within him.

Isaiah 42:5 Thus saith God the LORD, he that created the heavens, and stretched them out; he that spread forth the earth, and that which cometh out of it; he that giveth breath unto the people upon it, and spirit to them that walk therein.

Isaiah 45:12 I have made the earth, and created man upon it: I, even my hands, have stretched out the heavens, and all their host have I commanded.

Jeremiah 10:12 He hath made the earth by his power, he hath established the world by his wisdom, and hath stretched out the heavens by his discretion.

Job 9:8 Which alone spreadeth out the heavens, and treadeth upon the waves of the sea.

Psalm 104:2 Who coverest thyself with light as with a garment: who stretchest out the heavens like a curtain.

Isaiah 51:13 And forgettest the LORD thy maker, that hath stretched forth the heavens, and laid the foundations of the earth; and hast feared continually every day because of the fury of the oppressor, as if he were ready to destroy? and where is the fury of the oppressor?

Jeremiah 51:15 He hath made the earth by his power, he hath established the world by his wisdom, and hath stretched out the heaven by his understanding.

> *O LORD our Lord, how excellent is thy name in all the earth!*
> WHO HAST SET THY GLORY ABOVE THE HEAVENS.
> PSALM 8:1

The Hubble Space Telescope has imaged striking details of the famed planetary nebula designated NGC 2818. This spectacular structure contains the outer layers of a star that were expelled into interstellar space. As strongly as God's glory is reflected in such beauties spread across the comos, yet God Himself far supersedes all that He has made.

THE MESSAGE GIVER   13

"Some label it the UNIVERSE, others name it the COSMOS, some entitle it the HEAVENS, and others simply call it SPACE, but the term that fits best is the **GLORY OF GOD!**"

This supersized, 340–megapixel image of the center of the Milky Way Galaxy shows the innumerable stars that band together to create the glow that's visible on a clear night. The dark band is not an area devoid of stars, but an area filled with interstellar dust that obscures the view of stars in the background. It covers an area of sky that would appear slightly larger than a fully opened hand held at arm's length. In the upper left corner, the small pink patch with a blue haze directly above it is the Trifid Nebula. A close–up image of this nebula can be seen on page 116.

THE MESSAGE GIVER   15

 *Greater than the greatness of all mysteries of creation* **is the greatness of God above all the mysterious things He created.**

years that this also was false. Job 26:7 says, "He stretcheth out the north over the empty place, and hangeth the earth upon nothing."

For millennia it was thought that the sun and stars rotated around the earth once every 24 hours as they appear to us from our perspective on Earth. It was believed that the earth was stationary. The modern understanding, of course, is that the *earth* is rotating and giving the *illusion* that the heavenly bodies orbit the earth once every 24 hours. The Bible confirmed this in Job 38, verses 12 and 14, long before it was proposed by Nicolaus Copernicus: "Hast thou commanded the morning since thy days; and caused the dayspring to know his place; That it might take hold of the ends of the earth . . . It is turned as clay to the seal; and they stand as a garment." The picture of the earth turning as clay before a potter indicates the earth's rotating motion.

The most firmly established natural law in science confirms a "finished" creation. Genesis 2:1 states, "Thus the heavens and the earth were finished, and all the host of them." This shows that when the six days were completed, all the initial work on creation was finished. This was not expressed by philosophers until modern times, when the first law of thermodynamics was formulated. This law states that the total quantity of all matter and energy in the universe is a constant; nothing is being added or taken away.[3] In the Bible, the Creator also says that the universe is deteriorating. This was confirmed by the second law of thermodynamics, which states that all systems in the universe, when left to themselves, tend to become disordered, dispersed, and corrupted, decaying into a form of disintegrated chaos.[4] This was not acknowledged by man until 2,500 years after it was initially revealed in the Bible where it speaks of the earth "wax[ing] old like a garment" (Isaiah 51:6; Psalm 102:26; Hebrews 1:10, 11).[b] This law also shows that the evolutionary theory of the continual betterment of our universe with no outside influence is completely at odds with the laws of physics.

God's Word is accurate and can be trusted in scientific as well as spiritual matters. The Bible has been right all along, and human discoveries have been slowly catching up to the many exciting truths revealed in God's Word. Contrary to what some would say, the Bible and science are compatible with each other. God is the author of science and has created everything, including all the laws of physics, so we can expect to see creation align with the Word of God in beautiful harmony.

---

[b] Isaiah 51:6 Lift up your eyes to the heavens, and look upon the earth beneath: for the heavens shall vanish away like smoke, and the earth shall wax old like a garment, and they that dwell therein shall die in like manner: but my salvation shall be forever, and my righteousness shall not be abolished.

Psalm 102:26 They shall perish, but thou shalt endure: yea, all of them shall wax old like a garment; as a vesture shalt thou change them, and they shall be changed.

Hebrew 1:10-11 And, Thou, Lord, in the beginning hast laid the foundation of the earth; and the heavens are the works of thine hands: They shall perish; but thou remainest; and they all shall wax old as doth a garment.

God intends us to enjoy His creation; *that's why it's beautiful.* We see His wonders above us, beneath us, all around us, even within us. We're encircled by an eye-popping, mind-boggling, awe-inspiring cosmos, *which logically implies there's a Creator who sees, thinks, and inspires awe.* The universe is full of pulsating energy, so its Maker must be *omnipotent*. It appears virtually endless, so He must be *eternal*. Because it's finely calibrated, He must be *intelligent*. Since it contains life, He must be *personal*; and since it's magnificent, He must be *altogether lovely*. Assuming the existence of a CREATOR isn't a mindless leap of faith; **it's the most reasonable thing in the universe.**

ROBERT MORGAN

By the word of the Lord were the heavens made;

AND ALL THE HOST OF THEM BY THE BREATH OF HIS MOUTH. PSALM 33:6

The heavens were formed by the word of the Lord, and as Psalm 33:6 says, by the "breath of His mouth." What a fitting description for the creation of this stunning cloud of stars; it could almost look as if it were a vapor cloud breathed from the Creator's mouth. This cluster, known as M54, holds thousands of stars that are gravitationally bound together. In the same way that God created them, He is still "upholding all things by the word of his power" (Hebrews 1:3).

chapter two
The Message Bearers

THE SUN

Far off in space, massive and incredibly powerful objects wreak havoc on everything nearby. They have been blazing throughout history and give no indication of letting up anytime soon. Churning with violent nuclear forces within and extreme heat and magnetism without, these monsters are kept millions of miles away from us to ensure our safety. We call these giants *stars*.

Man has wondered for thousands of years what the stars actually are. Their extreme distance has made it difficult to learn anything about them until the recent advances of technology. The stars are so far away that we can't really discern their true nature by casually looking at them. Their distance causes them to appear quiet and gentle, but in reality they are extremely powerful, aggressively generating intense heat and light.

One of these stars is much closer to us than all the others; we call it the sun. It is just the right distance from Earth to support life. By observing the sun, we can learn what the other stars may be like. The sun is composed mainly of hydrogen and helium. Neither a solid or gas, the sun consists of plasma. This plasma is tenuous and gaseous near the surface but gets denser closer to the sun's core. Most astronomers believe it produces energy by way of **nuclear fusion** processes in the core, where hydrogen nuclei are fused together to form helium. This is the same process that takes place within nuclear bombs, and this is what enables the sun and stars to generate heat and light. In spite of these powerful forces raging in their interiors, gravity enables the sun and other stars to maintain the appearance of spheres.

The earth receives only a tiny fraction of the sun's total energy, only about one-half of a billionth of the energy poured out in all directions.[1] Yet the amount of solar energy we receive on the earth in one hour is great enough that if we could harness it all, it would be enough to power all the cities and homes around the world for an entire year. The sun produces as much energy every second as 20 billion hydrogen bombs. These are the largest of all bombs, much more powerful than any atomic bomb ever used in warfare. A hydrogen bomb is about 1,000 times more powerful than the atomic bombs used in Japan during World War II.[2, 3]

Occasionally a solar storm erupts on the surface of the sun. These can be so intense that the charged particles released in the storm affect satellites orbiting the earth. Solar storms result from the sun's irregular rotation. Because the sun is not solid like the earth, its poles rotate at a different rate than its equator. Near the poles the rate of one complete rotation is about 33 days, whereas the equator of the sun rotates in about 26 days. The sun has **magnetic field** lines running from pole to pole like the earth does. Because these field lines are rotating at different rates, they sometimes tangle. Where these electromagnetic tangles occur, the intense magnetism creates cooler areas on the sun's surface.

Extreme Ultraviolet Imaging Telescope (EIT) image of a huge, handle-shaped prominence. Prominences are huge clouds of relatively cool, dense plasma suspended in the sun's hot, thin corona. At times they can erupt, escaping the sun's atmosphere. The hottest areas appear almost white, while the darker red areas indicate cooler temperatures.

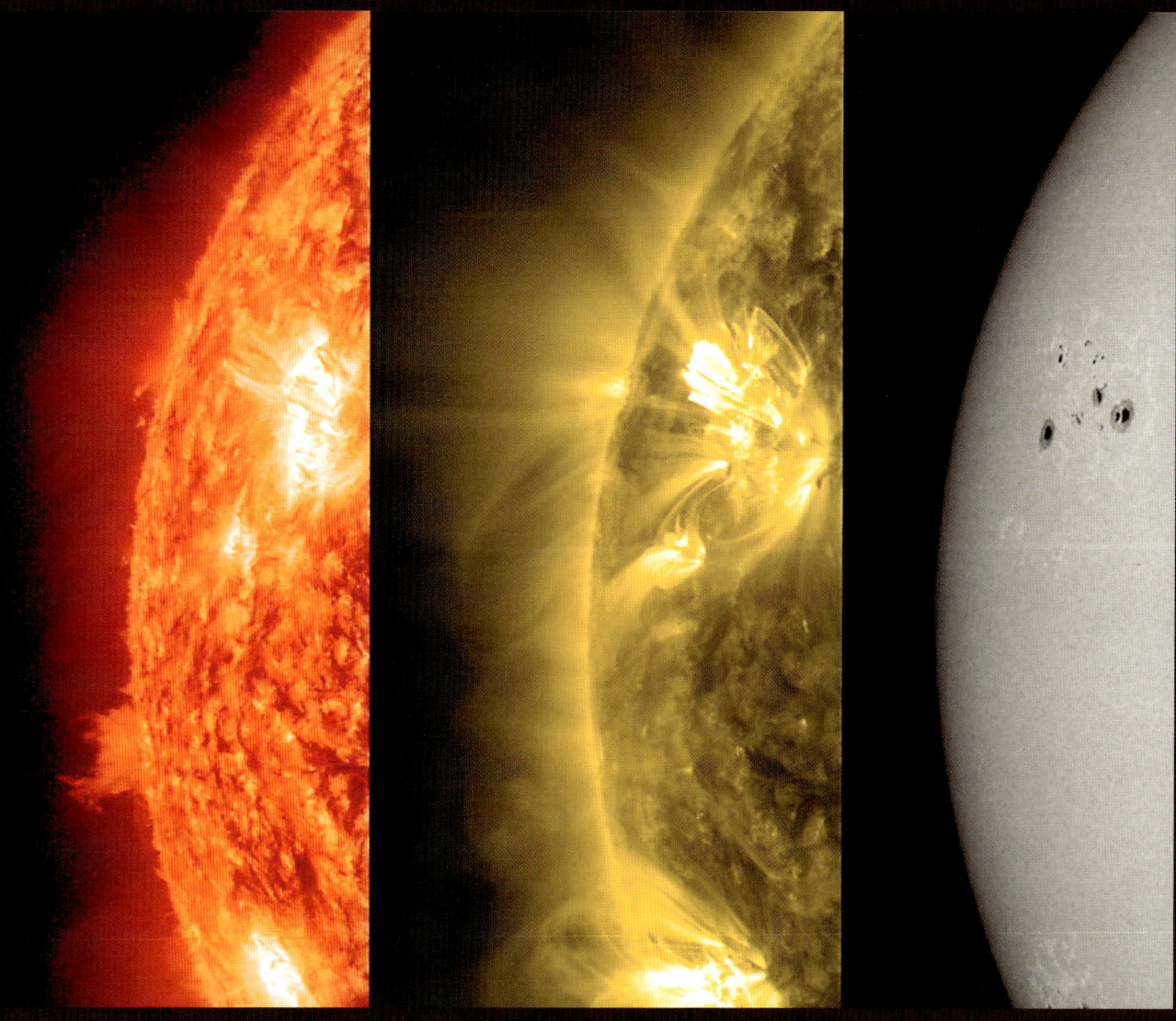

A pair of dynamic active regions rotated into view as the Solar Dynamics Observatory (SDO) caught the activity for a little over two days (August 15-17, 2011). One can compare the activity in this side-by-side-by-side photograph in three wavelengths. On the left, plasma on the sun's surface is shown at 60,000 degrees Fahrenheit in extreme ultraviolet light. The feature rising up above the sun's edge between the active regions is a prominence. The middle image with its many looping arcs, also in extreme ultraviolet light, shows plasma in the sun's atmosphere, heated to about a million degrees. The right image shows the source of all the activity—magnetically intense sunspots on the sun's surface.

THE MESSAGE BEARERS 23

Sunspots

One of the largest sunspots ever recorded shows up in the lower portion of this image of the sun. The spot's area was about 15 times the size of Earth. This same sunspot released an X-class flare that was among the largest ever seen and unleashed a fast-moving coronal mass ejection.

These areas appear darker and are called sunspots. As the magnetic field lines continue their struggle to untangle, they can cause two types of storms. One is a solar flare. The other is more energetic and caused by the ejection of **mass** away from the sun when the field lines break. This is called a coronal mass ejection (CME). In such an explosion, the sun can throw off billions of tons of matter into space. If the speed of this ejection of mass is high enough and if the mass is moving in the right direction, it can interact with Earth's magnetic field. In such cases, we see the aurora borealis, also known as northern lights. In addition, these ejections can interact with satellites, cell phone communication, the electrical grid, and navigational systems for ships, planes, or cars.

One solar storm happened at 9:00 p.m. Eastern Daylight Time on October 21, 2011. The sun's magnetic field lines had been twisted and distorted out of their normal pattern. This caused a coronal mass ejection (CME). A segment of the magnetic field lines was broken, releasing an explosive torrent of stellar material consisting of plasma and charged particles. This time the blast was directed toward the earth. The cloud of charged particles, traveling at over two million miles per hour, reached the earth 41 hours later. Thankfully, the earth's magnetic field got in the way and shielded us from most of the harmful particles. However, the CME had released a knot of particles with south-pointing magnetic fields that partially canceled the earth's north-pointing magnetic field at the equator, allowing the solar wind to penetrate more deeply than normal into the earth's magnetosphere. The particles blasted in toward the polar regions, knocking off electrons from atoms that make up our atmosphere. This ignited a blaze of northern lights seen as far south as the southern United States. From there they appeared as a red glow that extended up from the northern horizon. Vertical streaks would form and last a couple of minutes, only to fade away and be replaced by others.

A CME might seem like a violent anomaly from our seemingly tranquil sun, but it actually occurs about once a day on average. However, only the high energy ones that are earth-directed cause intense disturbances in the earth's atmosphere.

The most severe solar storm on record happened in 1859. Telegraph operators reported being literally shocked by their instruments. Even after

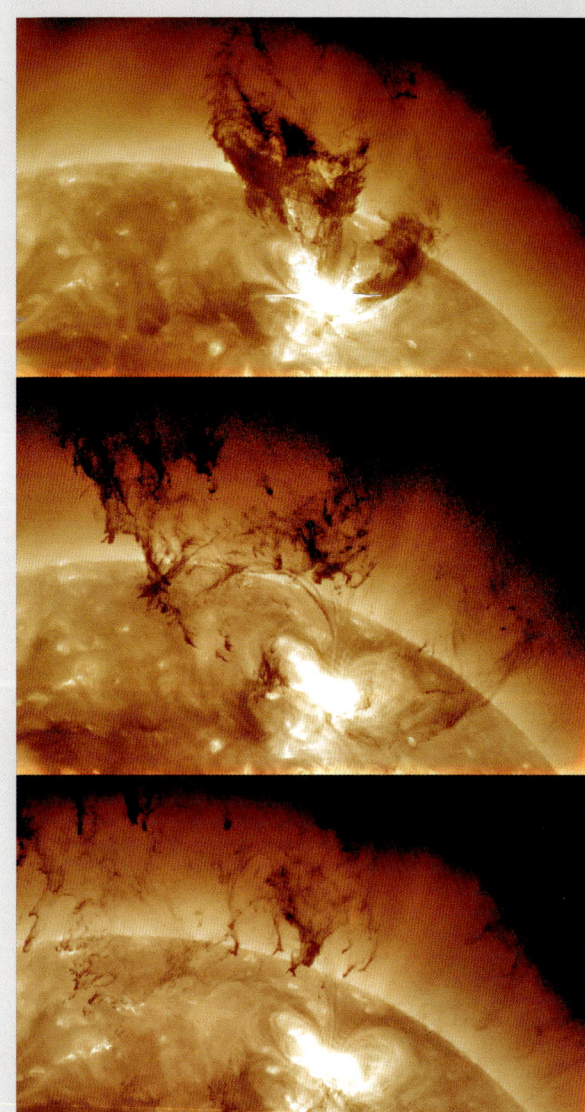

On June 7, 2011, the sun unleashed an M-2 (medium-sized) solar flare (white flash in the first image) with a spectacular coronal mass ejection (the darker material). The large cloud of particles mushroomed up and fell back down, looking as if it covered an area almost half the solar surface.

THE MESSAGE BEARERS   25

Space Weather Essentials

1. Sun unleashes solar storm.

2. Coronal mass ejection bursts into space.

3. Earth's magnetosphere at times gets hit with charged particles.

4. Our atmosphere glows with auror lights (seen from Earth and space).

5. Charged particles affect communications, navigation, satellites, the power grids, more.

Above: The aurora borealis, also known as northern lights, are seen lighting up the night sky over Bear Lake in Alaska. These lights are a direct result of activity on the sun that influences our atmosphere.

Left: This illustration shows a coronal mass ejection (CME) blasting off the sun's surface in the direction of Earth. Such storms can produce aurora effects in the earth's atmosphere that are visible in the night sky on Earth.

THE MESSAGE BEARERS 27

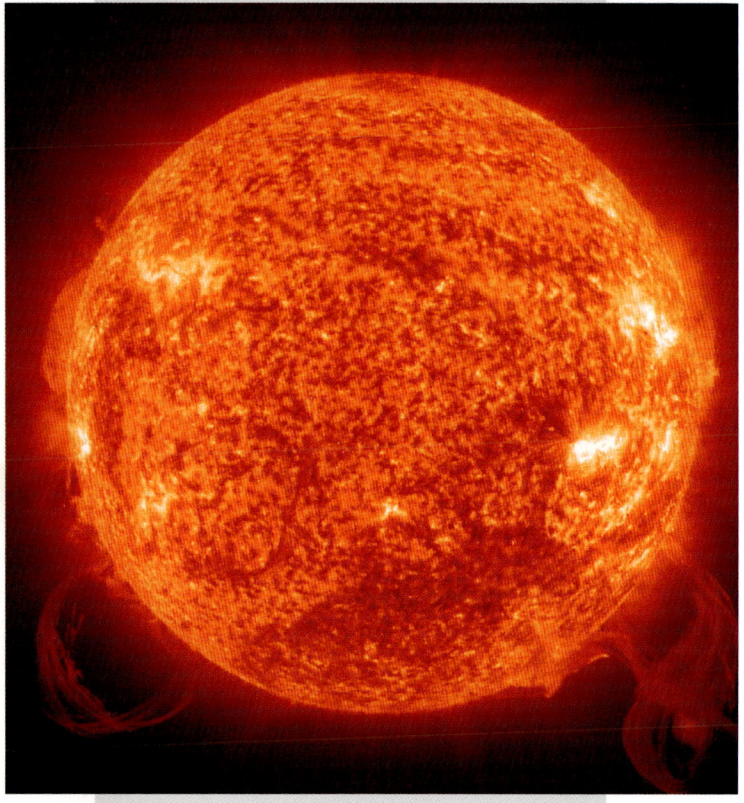

The appearance of two large prominences in one image makes this one of the most spectacular images of the sun that has been captured. For a sense of scale, the prominences extend the distance of about 20 Earths out from the sun.

unhooking the instruments from the power supply, messages could still be transmitted, powered only by the currents in the atmosphere that had been caused by the sun over 90 million miles away.

The following report from NASA details what could happen if another such storm would strike today.

> The 1859 storm—known as the "Carrington Event" after astronomer Richard Carrington who witnessed the instigating solar flare—electrified transmission cables, set fires in telegraph offices, and produced northern lights so bright that people could read newspapers by their red and green glow. A recent report by the National Academy of Sciences found that if a similar storm occurred today, it could cause 1 to 2 trillion dollars in damages to society's high-tech infrastructure and require 4 to 10 years for complete recovery. For comparison, Hurricane Katrina caused "only" 80 to 125 billion dollars in damage.[4]

Contrary to how it may appear from Earth, the sun is not the powerhouse of the universe. The only reason it appears so much bigger and brighter than the other stars is that it's much closer to Earth. The next closest stars are over 250,000 times farther away from us than the sun! Yet the sun is so large that if we would weigh the **solar system,** 99 percent of the total weight would consist of the sun, and the remaining 1 percent would be the combined weight of all the planets, moons, asteroids, comets, and meteoroids. Though the sun is relatively close, its distance is still far enough that light, traveling at 670,617,000 miles per hour, takes eight minutes to reach the earth. If the sun would instantly turn off, we wouldn't realize it until eight minutes later when the last light rays would reach the earth.

Although the sun and the moon appear almost exactly the same size from Earth, in reality there is no comparison. If the sun and the moon would exchange locations, the moon would appear to be 400 times smaller and look like only a dim star. The sun would completely engulf the space where Earth is and extend beyond it 190,000 additional miles!

28   THE CELESTIAL MESSAGE

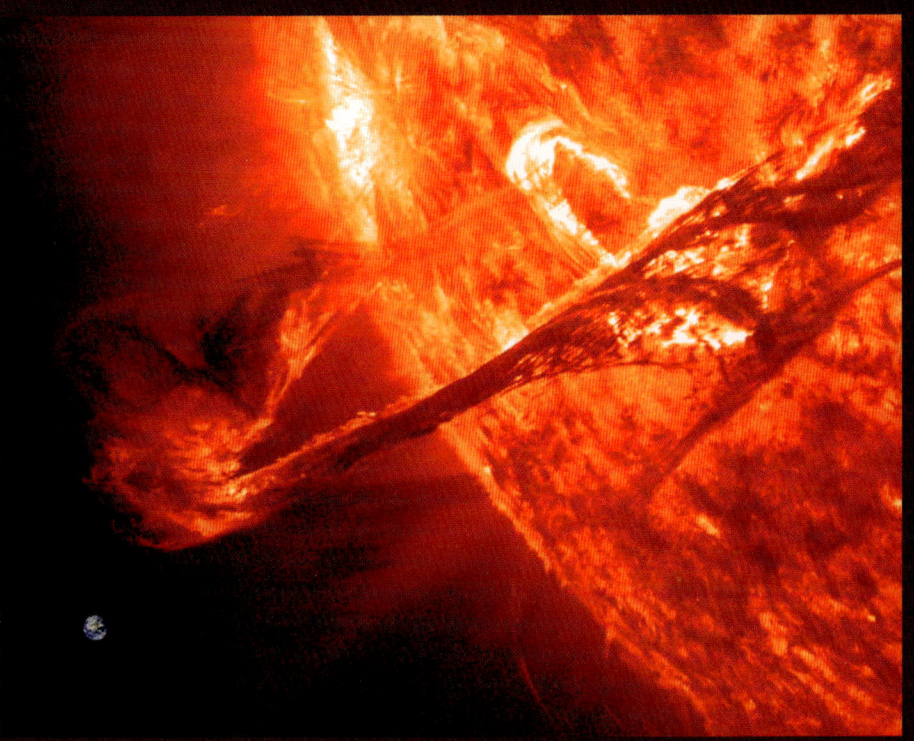 

On August 31, 2012, a medium-sized flare burst off the sun and triggered a long filament of solar plasma that was ejected from the surface in an enormous, violent eruption. Some of the solar material seen here went on to collide with the earth, generating beautiful auroras. The earth is shown here sized to scale with respect to the sun and placed on the image to give a dramatic sense of the magnitude of this outburst. However, the earth is not actually this close to the sun. In reality, it is nearly 700 times farther away.

This solar active region offers a beautiful profile view of cascading loops spiraling above it following a solar flare eruption (January 15–16, 2012). These loop structures, just one of which is the size of several Earths, are made of superheated plasma.

THE MESSAGE BEARERS

THE STARS
The Far-Flung Frontier

As numbers roll ever higher, our understanding of them decreases. It's not uncommon to encounter numbers that stretch our comprehensive ability to the breaking point. This makes it difficult to try to grasp the distances across the universe or comprehend the size of objects in it. Learning about the universe carries with it the side effect of being inundated with a steady barrage of literally astronomical numbers. It helps us get a handle on the significance of these numerical giants, however, if we compare them to familiar objects.

For example, we know the number 93 million, the number of miles between the sun and the earth, sounds big, but it's too big to really mean anything to us. To help us conceptualize this number, if that same number of people would stand in a row, tightly packed shoulder to shoulder, the line would encircle the entire earth.

The number that expresses the size of the sun also stretches the imagination. Flying a jet at 600 miles per hour from the surface of the sun to its center would take a month of nonstop travel to cover the entire 432,000 miles—and that's just the radius of the sun!

Earlier we mentioned Proxima Centauri, the nearest star to the earth after the sun. It is over 24 trillion miles away. If we would have that number of people stand shoulder to shoulder, the line would wrap around the earth 258,000 times. A stack of 24 trillion dollar bills would reach all the way to the moon, circle it 150 times, and come all the way back again. Still lost? Maybe this will help: we could make a pile of 24 trillion feathers and put them on a scale. They would weigh approximately 12 million tons.

From the center of our Milky Way Galaxy, the earth lies about two-thirds of the way out to the galaxy's edge. This distance is about 159 quadrillion miles. If it were possible to take that same number of hairs and have them packed tightly side by side, the line would extend for

Omega Centauri

The core of the spectacular globular cluster Omega Centauri glitters with the combined light of two million stars. The entire cluster contains 10 million stars and is among the most massive of some 200 globular clusters orbiting the Milky Way Galaxy.

THE MESSAGE BEARERS   31

Whoever it was who
SEARCHED THE HEAVENS
with a telescope and found
no God would not have found
the human mind if he had
SEARCHED THE BRAIN
with a microscope.

GEORGE SANTAYANA

Andromeda Galaxy

The Andromeda Galaxy is the nearest major galaxy to the Milky Way at approximately 2.4 million **light-year**s away. It is the farthest object from Earth that can be seen with the naked eye. The diameter of the galaxy is 100,000 light-years, about the same as our Milky Way. To illustrate this stupendous size, a pinhole in a postcard-sized image of Andromeda would represent 600 light-years. Flying across those 600 light-years of space at the speed of a jet (600 miles per hour) would take over 650 million years.

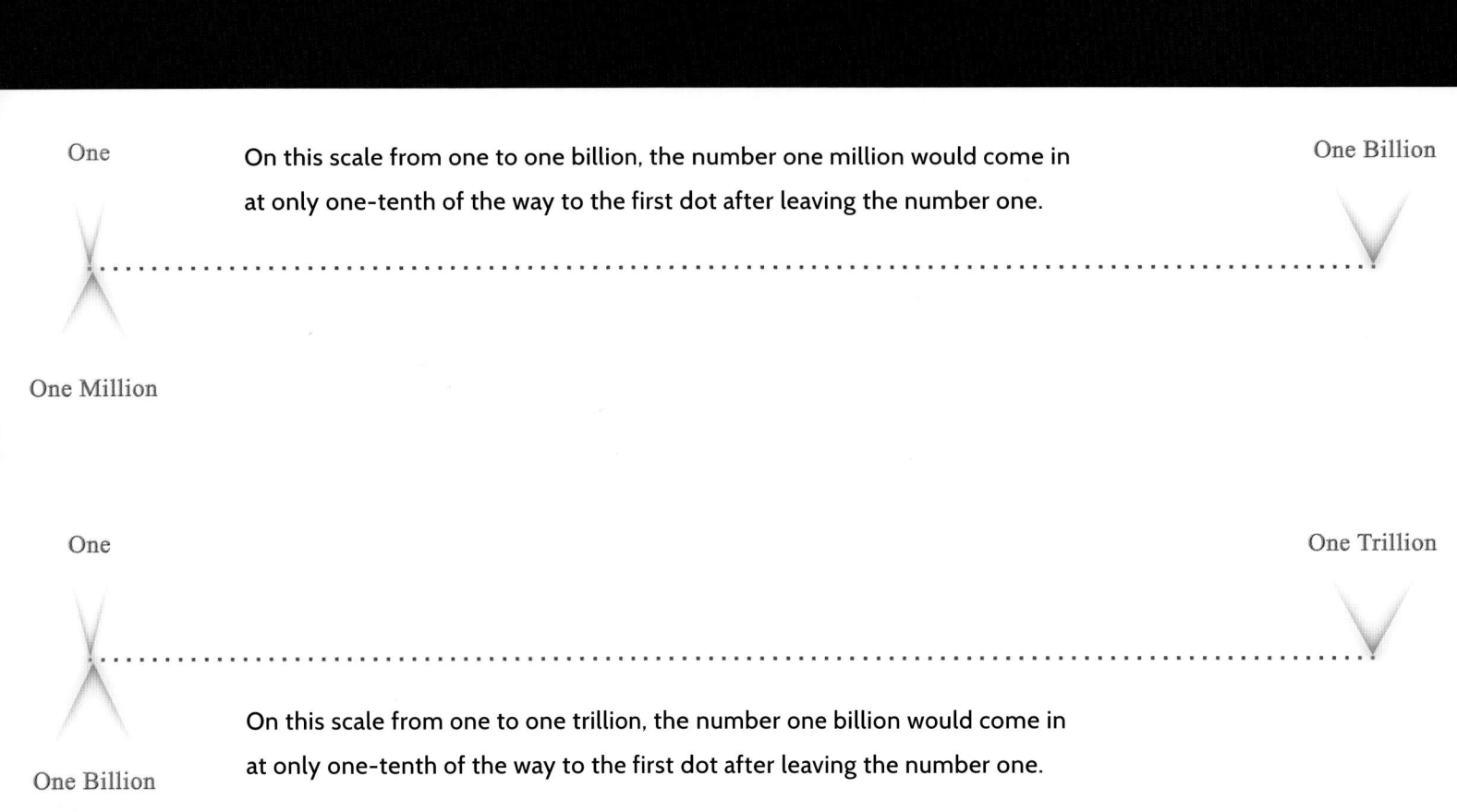

9.9 billion miles. Since that analogy is still difficult to connect with our experience, just imagine traveling down this row of hairs at 100 miles per hour. It would take more time than the entire history of the earth—more than 11,000 years.

As if that weren't hard enough to grasp, the distance to intergalactic space is even farther! To get to the nearest major galaxy, Andromeda, we would have to travel 88 times farther than the distance from Earth to the center of our Milky Way, a calculator-busting distance of 14,108,411,189,256,000,000 miles. To get to some of the most distant galaxies we can see, we'd need to go 5,000 times farther than Andromeda, but to try to comprehend that mind-numbing distance is simply futile.

Just as we would never talk of driving 316,000 inches to a grocery store if it were five miles away, astronomers would never speak of looking 14 quintillion miles out to the Andromeda Galaxy. Astronomers deal with these astronomical numbers by using units of measurement that are much larger than miles. The most familiar of these is a light-year. One light-year is the distance light travels in one year as it blazes along at 186,000 miles per second. The distance is equal to almost 6 trillion miles. With this unit of measurement, the distance to Andromeda can be expressed in a much more manageable term of 2.5 million light-years.

One well-known way to help understand the significance of large numbers is to compare them with units of time. One million seconds in the past was 11 days ago. One billion seconds ago was almost 32 years in the past. One trillion seconds back in history was about 26,000 years before the world began—32,000 years ago.

Man has been to the moon, and spacecraft have explored the planets and studied the sun. But will man ever visit the stars? Not very likely, unless we mimic the migrations of the monarch butterfly, whose journeys take entire generations of time. The stars are so far away that if we would spend an entire lifetime of 100 years traveling at one million miles per hour, which is 27 times faster than any spacecraft has ever traveled, we would travel only 1/27 of the way to the nearest star![5]

Another way to help us understand the tremendous distances between the earth and the stars is to shrink everything down to a more manageable size. If we were to make everything in the universe 10 billion times smaller, Earth would be down to the size of a pinhead, less than 1/16 of an inch across. At this scale, the moon would be less than 1/64 of an inch in diameter and would be 1½ inches away from Earth. The sun would be about 5½ inches in diameter and would be about 49 feet in the distance. The planet Jupiter would be 255 feet away from Earth and the dwarf planet Pluto almost 2,000 feet. But the big jump comes in calculating the distance to the nearest star. Proxima Centauri would be 2,470 miles away, which is about the distance across the United States. In our analogy, the entire Milky Way Galaxy would stretch across 58.8 million miles of space, and the sun would be about 15.8 million miles away from the center of the galaxy.

Continuing with a scaled down model, where everything has been shrunk to 10 billion times its normal size, we'll move out to the Andromeda Galaxy. It would lie 1.5 billion miles from Earth, 16 times farther than the actual distance from Earth to the sun. And beyond that, one of the most distant galaxies in the universe is so far away that even in our scale of 1 to 10 billion, it would be 8 trillion, 53 billion, 551 million miles away.

To put the number 8 trillion into proper perspective, let's imagine making a stack of that many one-dollar bills. One bill is about one-tenth of a millimeter thick, so it would take over 3,000 bills to make a stack one foot high. To make the stack a mile high, we would need over 16 million bills. We could make it all the way to the moon with a little over 3.8 trillion bills. So with 8 trillion of them, we could cover the distance of over 238,000 miles to the moon, come all the way back to Earth, and still have 400 billion dollars to spare.

We are faced with such an unimaginable distance even after we shrink the universe by a factor of 10 billion. This leaves us confounded by its enormous size, but Isaiah wrote that God has "meted out heaven with the span." Whether literally or otherwise, God can, in some way, measure out the universe with His hand breadth.

For as the heavens are higher than the earth, SO ARE MY WAYS HIGHER THAN YOUR WAYS, AND MY THOUGHTS THAN YOUR THOUGHTS. ISAIAH 55:9

For as the heaven is high above the earth, SO GREAT IS HIS MERCY toward them that *fear him.* PSALM 103:11

Who hath . . . *meted out heaven with the span.* ISAIAH 40:12

Is not God in the height of heaven?
**and behold the height of the stars,
how high they are!** JOB 22:12

Celestial Behemoths

Because of their extreme distance from Earth, stars appear to be tiny flickers of light in the sky that could almost be snuffed out by a breeze on a summer night. But stars are not what they appear to be. Though we travel across approximately 180 million miles of space every year as the earth orbits the sun, the stars do not appear to get brighter or larger when we get closer to them. This indicates their extreme distance, not their size!

Perhaps by comparing the stars to the earth, we can grasp a bit of their enormity. Let's start with Earth and shrink it down to one inch in diameter, about the size of a quarter. At this scale the planet Uranus would be four inches tall and about the size of a softball. Jupiter, the largest planet in our solar system, would be 11 inches in diameter, just a little larger than a basketball.

But even though some of the planets are extremely large, they are dwarfed by the stars. In our scaled-down comparison, the sun would be nine feet tall and therefore could not fit in a standard house with eight-foot ceilings. And, as we know, there are other stars that are much larger than the sun. The brightest star as seen from Earth is called Sirius. In our analogy it would be almost 16 feet tall.

Another **giant** star in our neighborhood is Arcturus. It would measure 234 feet, making it about as high as a cellular communications broadcasting tower. If that isn't enough to amaze you, consider Rigel. This **supergiant** star would be over 700 feet in diameter, more than twice as high as the Statue of Liberty.

Moving into the category of supergiants, we come to a star called Betelgeuse. With the scale we've been using, Betelgeuse would be 10,000 feet high. This would equal the height of close to seven of the historic twin towers on top of each other. And then, as if we needed to have something to stretch our minds even more, God created VY Canis Majoris. Continuing with our scale, with Earth the size of a quarter, this **hypergiant** star, VY Canis Majoris, would be nearly three miles high. More than 11 of the twin towers would need to be stacked together to equal this height.

The next time you see a star twinkling silently in the night, just think of the giant it must be to enable it to be seen from trillions of miles away.

Sun   Sirius

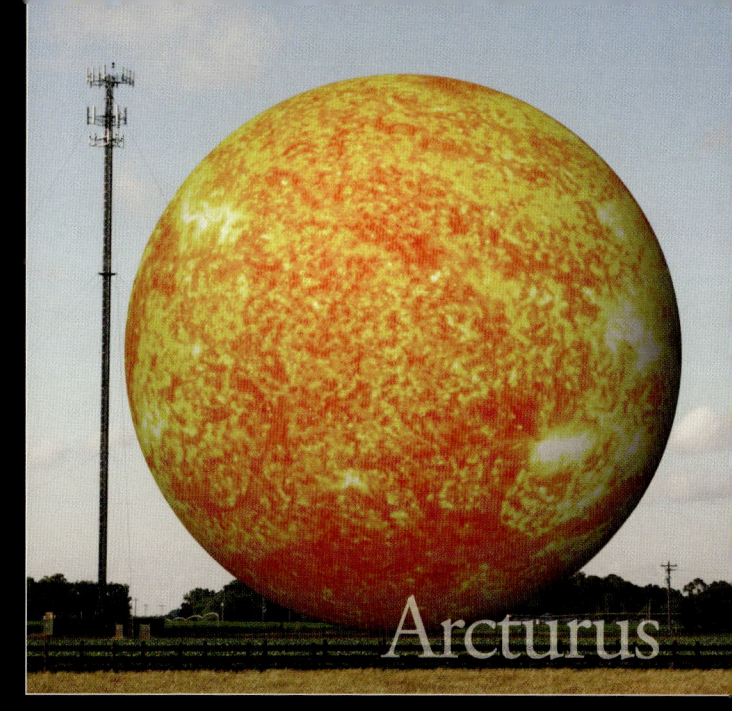

Arcturus

Rigel

Betelgeuse

These illustrations compare the relative sizes of the planets, sun, and some of the stars in our galaxy.

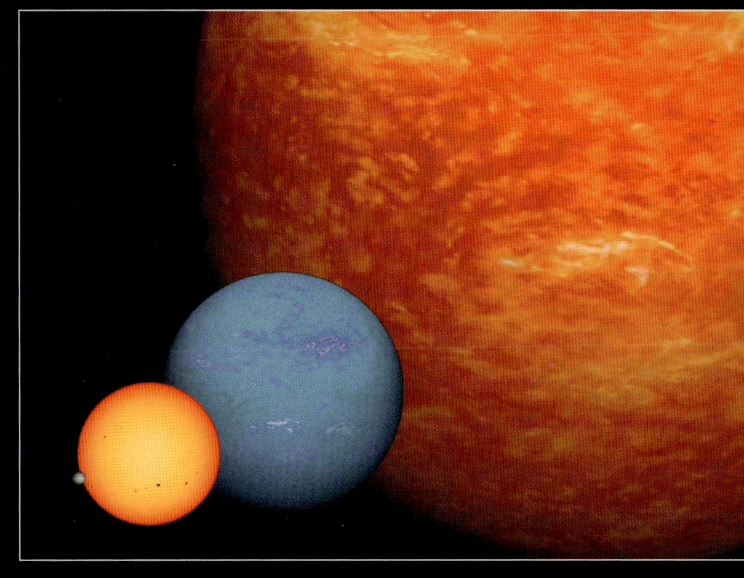

ERCURY   MARS   VENUS   EARTH   NEPTUNE   URANUS   SATURN   JUPITER

JUPITER   SUN   SIRIUS   POLLUX

POLLUX   ARCTURUS   ALDEBARAN   RIGEL

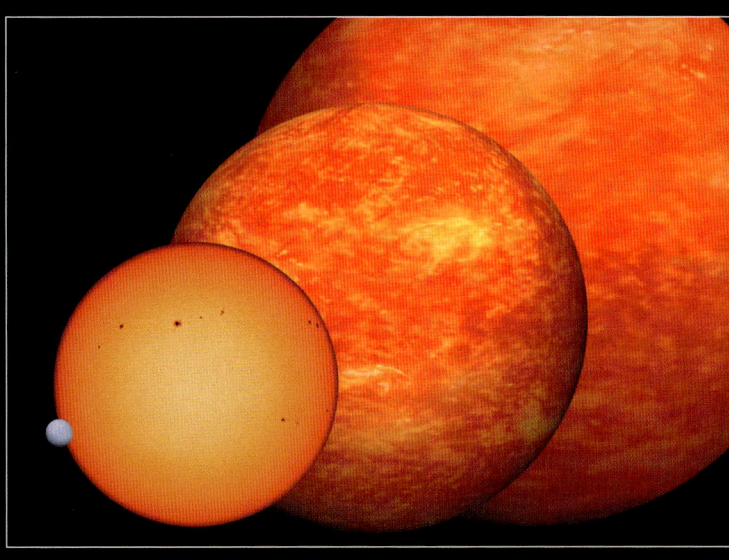

RIGEL   ANTARES   BETELGEUSE   VY CANIS MAJORIS

40   THE CELESTIAL MESSAGE

Astronomers have studied VY Canis Majoris for more than a century. The star is located 5,000 light-years away. It is 500,000 times brighter and 30 to 40 times more massive than the sun. If the sun were replaced with the bloated VY Canis Majoris, its surface could extend to the orbit of Saturn. VY Canis Majoris is a red supergiant. A massive star becomes a red supergiant near the end of its life when it exhausts the hydrogen fuel at its core. As the core contracts under gravity, the outer layers expand and become less dense. As a result, the highly unstable star gets 100 times larger, and it begins to expel mass at a higher rate. VY Canis Majoris has probably already shed about half of its mass, and it will eventually explode.

VY Canis Majoris

Sun

A comparison of the relative sizes of the sun and Canis Majoris. The dot that represents the sun could be filled with one million Earths.

THE MESSAGE BEARERS   41

This stellar swarm is M80, one of the densest of the globular star clusters in the Milky Way Galaxy. Located about 28,000 light-years from Earth, M80 contains hundreds of thousands of stars, all held together by their mutual gravitational attraction.

Superpowers

For the sake of better understanding the magnitude of energy coming from these stars, we'll consider first a small star called a white dwarf. This particular type of star is much smaller than the sun and only slightly larger than the earth. However, its mass is about 200,000 times greater than the earth's. The energy it produces in one second would satisfy the electrical needs of the earth for 10,000 years.

The sun is much larger and more powerful than a white dwarf, shining about 100 times brighter. The amount of energy released by the sun in one second is equal to the amount of energy that 2.5 billion of the largest power plants on the earth could produce in an entire year.

The sun's total energy output is 380 septillion watts.[a] Converting the watts into horsepower gives a total figure of 500,000,000,000,000,000,000,000 (500 billion trillion) horsepower! How much power is that unimaginable amount? NASA[b] says it's enough energy to melt a bridge of ice two miles wide, one mile thick and extending the entire way from the earth to the sun, in one second.[6]

Although the sun is extremely powerful, the Pistol Star in the "supergiant" category is even more so, making the sun look like a damp firecracker in comparison. Situated in our neighborhood, in the Milky Way Galaxy, this star produces 10 million times more energy than the sun and gives off as much energy in six seconds as the sun does in an entire year.[7]

But when it comes to mind-bending amounts of energy, the

---

[a] Watts are based on an energy rate (one joule) per second.

[b] National Aeronautics and Space Administration

A series of active regions, lined up one after the other across the upper half of the sun, twisted and interacted with each other over 4½ days (September 28 – October 2, 2011). One of the leading active regions blasted out a coronal mass ejection, which was quickly succeeded by a blast from another active region. The disruption of the magnetic field from one likely triggered the second. Billions of tons of matter were ejected from the sun in these eruptions.

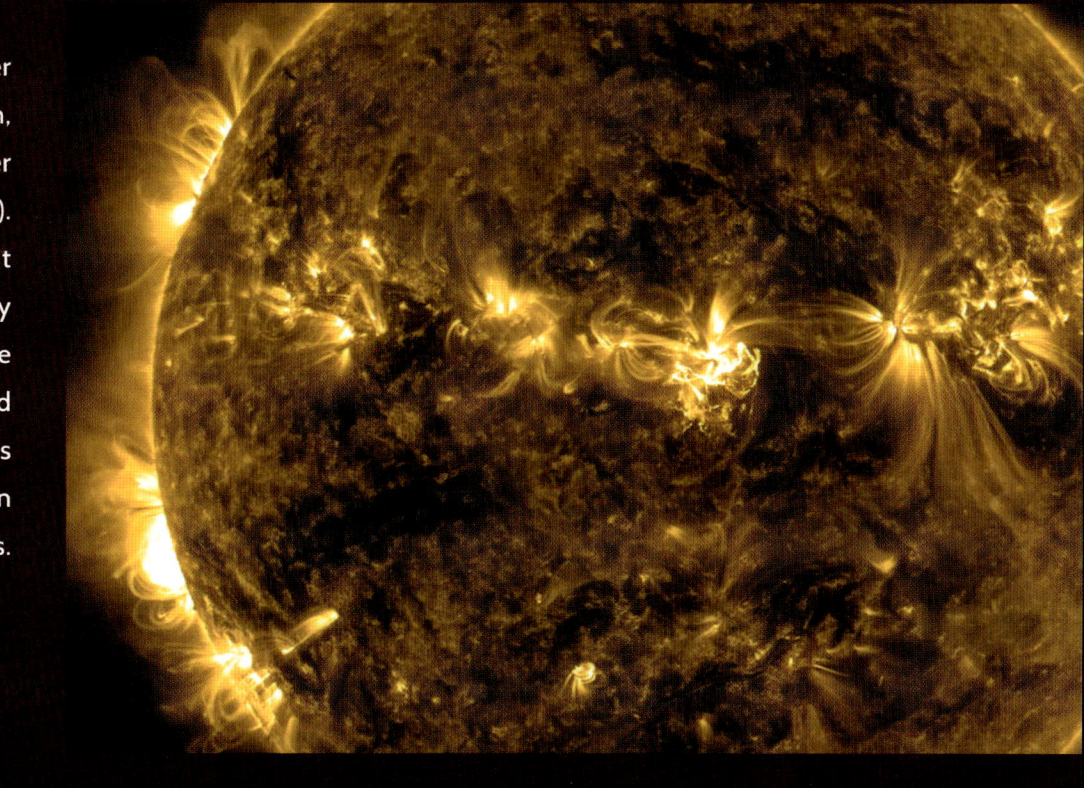

This spectacular coronal mass ejection shows the potential the sun has to suddenly release powerful bursts of energy. The cloud of plasma seen here was ejected off the surface of the sun and flung thousands of miles into space.

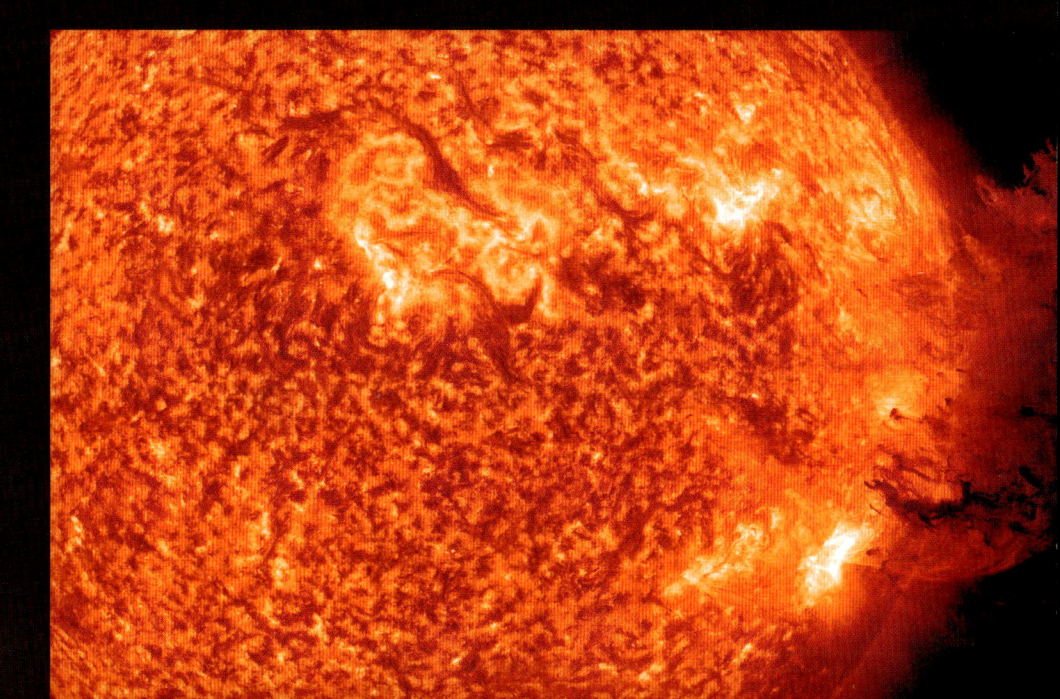

Astronomers using the Hubble telescope have identified what may be the most luminous star known, a celestial mammoth that releases up to 10 million times the energy of the sun and is big enough to fill the diameter of Earth's orbit. The Pistol Star, in the center of the image, unleashes as much energy in six seconds as our sun does in one year.

The image also shows one of the most massive eruptions ever seen in space. The star has enough raw power to blow off two expanding shells of gas equal to the mass of several of our suns. The largest shell is so big (four light-years), it could stretch nearly all the way from our sun to the next nearest star.

Despite shedding tremendous amounts of mass in these eruptions, astronomers estimate the extraordinary star may presently be 100 times more massive than our sun.

Pistol Star and all other stars have to move over to make room for quasars. Because of the incredible energy output of the quasars, it was hard for astronomers to know exactly what they were when they were first discovered.

Evidence shows now that quasars are powered by super-massive **black holes** at the centers of extremely active galaxies. The black holes exert a gravitational attractive force on everything around them that exceeds anything known on the earth. Whole stars can be arrested by their inescapable pull. Before a star even reaches a black hole, it is contorted beyond recognition as a result of the intense war between the outward kinetic energy from the star's blinding speed and the overwhelming inward gravitational pull of the black hole. Even light itself, however, cannot escape from a black hole's grip, and the black hole wins. The doomed star succumbs to being pulled apart, spaghettified, and ripped to shreds, forming an inward spiraling **accretion** disk around the black hole. Even solid objects like our planet Earth would be violently torn to pieces and sucked into the black hole if they got too close. As the matter in the disk spirals toward the ominous blackness, it releases huge amounts of energy and blinding light in a final desperate gasp before it becomes another morsel of the cosmic toast that feeds the voracious appetite of the insatiable black hole.

A quasar is the torrent of energy and radiation that surrounds a black hole and pours out from matter as it is being pulled through the accretion disk of a feeding black hole. In order for quasars to shine as brightly as they do, the black hole empowering them must consume the equivalent of several hundred thousand Earths or one whole star annually.[8] Astronomers tell us that a quasar is so powerful that it could outshine our entire galaxy, including the Pistol Star and all the other 100 billion stars combined, 100 times over.[9]

A casual glance into the star-studded night sky gives the illusion of peaceful tranquility. As we better understand the stars, however, we see the illusion for what it is. Tremendous amounts of energy are powering the heavens.

Quasars and black holes are not the only mysterious objects in the cosmos. Supernovas, pulsars, and others also make the list of bizarre celestial bodies. Although it's not very often that we get to see direct evidence of these things without the help of telescopes, a sighting did occur on July 4, A.D. 1054. On that day, a tremendous burst of starlight showered the earth and heralded the arrival of what appeared to be a new star in the sky.[10] Chinese astronomers dutifully recorded this historical event. A supernova explosion had occurred at a distance of 38 quadrillion miles away. However, the star had not just been born. It had been there all along, but its distance from Earth prohibited it from being seen until it obliterated itself in a violent outburst of light and energy. Even at this unimaginable distance, the explosion was still so bright that it could be seen in broad daylight, competing with the glaring sun. Shockwaves from the supernova blasted stardust and gases into a gigantic area of space measuring at least six light-years across. This is equal to 379,000 times the distance from the earth to the sun.

This widespread, ever-expanding conglomeration of stardust and gases is called the Crab Nebula today. Its quirky name comes from a drawing of the nebula made by Irish astronomer Lord Rosse in 1844. The supernova remnant is just a hollow shell reminding us of the cataclysmic explosion that ripped the original

An artist's concept of a quasar, seen at the center of a faraway galaxy

Streaming out from the center of the Galaxy M87 like a cosmic searchlight is one of nature's most amazing phenomena, a black-hole-powered jet of electrons and other sub-atomic particles traveling at nearly the speed of light. In this NASA Hubble Space Telescope image, the blue of the jet contrasts with the yellow glow from the combined light of billions of unseen stars and the yellow, point-like globular clusters that make up this galaxy. M87 has one of the nearest, most well-studied extragalactic jets, but many others exist. Wherever a massive black hole is feeding on a particularly rich diet of disrupted stars, gas, and dust, the conditions are right for the formation of a jet.

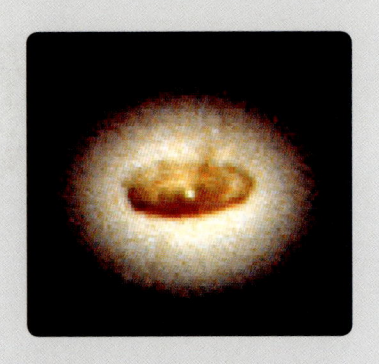

This is a Hubble Space Telescope image of an 800-light-year-wide spiral-shaped disk of dust spiraling into a massive black hole in the center of Galaxy NGC 4261. By measuring the speed of gas swirling around the black hole, astronomers calculate that the object at the center of the disk is 1.2 billion times the mass of our sun.

An artist's concept of matter swirling around a black hole.

> *There is one glory of the sun, and another glory of the moon, and another glory of the stars:* **for one star differeth from another star in glory.** 1 CORINTHIANS 15:41

powerful star to shreds.

At the center of the cloud of debris caused by a supernova explosion are the leftovers of the original star, forming a tightly compacted mass that weighs more than the sun, but is crushed down to the size of a large city. This rapidly spinning mass is known as a pulsar, which is a pulsating neutron star. The star at the center of the Crab Nebula is known as the Crab Pulsar. It flashes two beams of light toward the earth as it spins a full 30 times per second. Neutron stars are so densely compacted that one teaspoonful of neutron star material would weigh about a billion tons on the earth.[11]

Astronomers know of two possible scenarios that can cause a supernova to occur in a star. The first possibility is that a very hot and quickly burning star has used up all its lighter-weight fuels such as hydrogen and helium. Soon almost all that is left to burn is iron. Since iron doesn't burn very well in the process of nuclear fusion, the star's outwardly explosive force dramatically decreases. The core collapses in on itself before rebounding like a super ball into a massive explosion.

The second scenario occurs when two stars are very close together. If the mass of the one star is much greater than its companion, the greater star's stronger gravity overcomes the gravity of the lesser star and begins to pull away some of its mass (matter). This process is known as accretion. The pressure and temperature in the core then become so high that they start an uncontrollable nuclear chain reaction which detonates the star.

Galaxies can hold up to 100 billion stars or more. When a supernova occurs in one of these stars, it can single-handedly outshine the entire galaxy of billions of stars.

Crab Nebula

The Crab Nebula is a six-light-year-wide remnant of a star's supernova explosion that is still expanding. Japanese and Chinese astronomers recorded this violent event nearly 1,000 years ago in 1054.

Crab Pulsar

Left: Multiple observations made over several months with NASA's Chandra X-ray Observatory and the Hubble Space Telescope captured the spectacle of matter propelled to near the speed of light by the Crab Pulsar, a rapidly rotating neutron star the size of Manhattan. Bright wisps can be seen moving outward at half the speed of light to form an expanding ring that is visible in both X-ray and optical images.

Top: This image shows the entire region around Supernova 1987A. The most prominent feature in the image is a ring with dozens of bright spots. A shock wave of material unleashed by the stellar blast is slamming into the ring's inner regions, heating them up and causing them to glow.

Middle: A huge, billowing pair of gas and dust clouds are captured in this stunning NASA Hubble Space Telescope image of the supermassive star Eta Carinae. Estimated to be 100 times more massive than our sun, Eta Carinae may be one of the most massive stars in our galaxy. It radiates about five million times more power than the sun. This star had a giant outburst about 150 years ago, when it became one of the brightest stars in the southern sky. Though the star released as much visible light as a supernova explosion, it survived the outburst.

Bottom: This fascinating supernova remnant is known as SNR 0509-67.5. The explosion of the star was recorded nearly 400 years ago. The pink outer ring is plowing through space, expanding at more than 11 million miles per hour. It currently measures about 23 light-years across. The blue and green colors show heated star gas glowing in X-ray wavelengths of light like a giant stellar X-ray machine. These wavelengths are not a part of visible light and therefore could not be seen by the naked eye through a telescope.

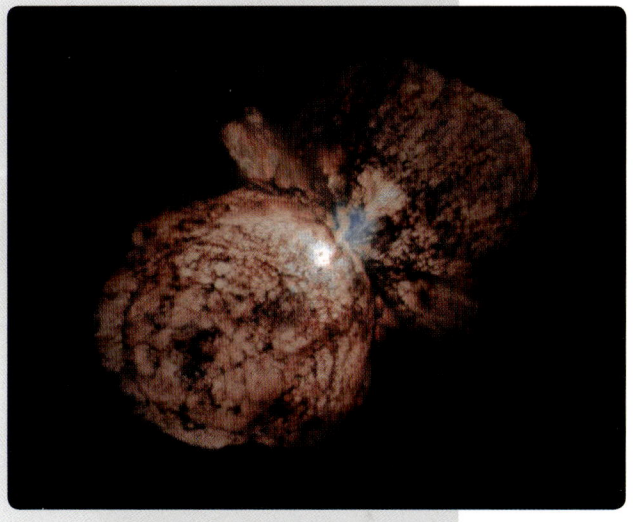

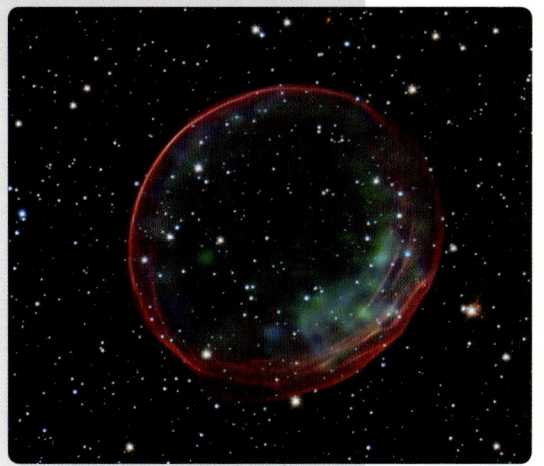

THE MESSAGE BEARERS   49

A ribbon of gas, a very thin section of a supernova remnant caused by a stellar explosion that occurred more than a thousand years ago, floats in our galaxy. The supernova that created it was probably the brightest star ever seen by humans.

When life becomes overwhelming, I step outside and lift my gaze to the heavens. **For I am convinced that the God who holds the stars in place will hold us through the night.**

SHEILA WALSH

O tell of HIS MIGHT, and sing of HIS GRACE, Whose robe is the light, **WHOSE CANOPY SPACE.**

ROBERT H. GRANT

The planets and dwarf planet Pluto are shown in their correct order from the sun, and their correct relative orbital distances. The sizes of the bodies are greatly exaggerated relative to the orbital distances.

chapter three
Parading Planets

The Creator has populated our solar system with other worlds somewhat similar to our own. The planets are not raging nuclear furnaces like the stars but are comparatively docile realms. Yet the natural state of all these neighbors is still very unnatural for us.

Venus is hot enough to melt lead and has clouds filled with sulfuric acid, the same highly corrosive acid used in vehicle batteries. It also has an atmosphere so thick and heavy that it puts 1,300 pounds of pressure on every square inch of the planet's surface.

The surface of Mars contains iron oxide, or rust, giving it a brown color. This planet also has a volcano three times higher than the tallest mountain on Earth and a canyon that cuts about five times deeper than the Grand Canyon.

Due to the methane gas in its atmosphere, Uranus sends off an odor like that of rotting animals. But if you could stand the smell, you would be in for a tremendous view: there are 27 moons and 9 rings stretching across its sky.

Jupiter spins so fast that it bulges around its equator. It is also an extremely massive planet. Because of its tremendous mass, humans as well as all other objects would be over twice as heavy on Jupiter as they are on Earth.

What did God have in mind when He created these otherworldly domains? Perhaps He felt satisfaction from sculpting surreal landscapes and filling them with the excitement of blasting winds or raging chemical oceans. Maybe He added a touch of class to Saturn by encircling it with a halo of dazzling rings in order to proclaim His glory and give us a window into His character. Could it be that the Author of such magnificent things is in reality quite exciting Himself? The solar system is packed with the exotic, wild, and wonderful. Is it possible that secular society's view of God as a monotonous, lackluster, arrogant ruler is completely wrong?

Absolutely! Our God is powerful and creative. Serving Him is not a trek through the desert. Rather, it is a journey through a garden of beauty where each turn unfolds new and extraordinary insights. This journey, the Christian life, is not based on emotion, but being in the presence of such an amazing God can be an awe-inspiring, spine-tingling experience.

MERCURY – THE SWIFT ONE

Mercury is the closest planet to the sun. At the place in its revolution where Mercury is nearest to the sun, the sun appears three times larger than it does from Earth. Mercury is a world of record-breaking extremes. It is the fastest of the planets, moving at a breakneck speed of about 112,000 miles per hour. It is also the smallest planet and has the slightest amount of gravity. It has the greatest range of temperature swings and the least amount of atmosphere. In fact, it has basically no atmosphere at all. The

Mercury

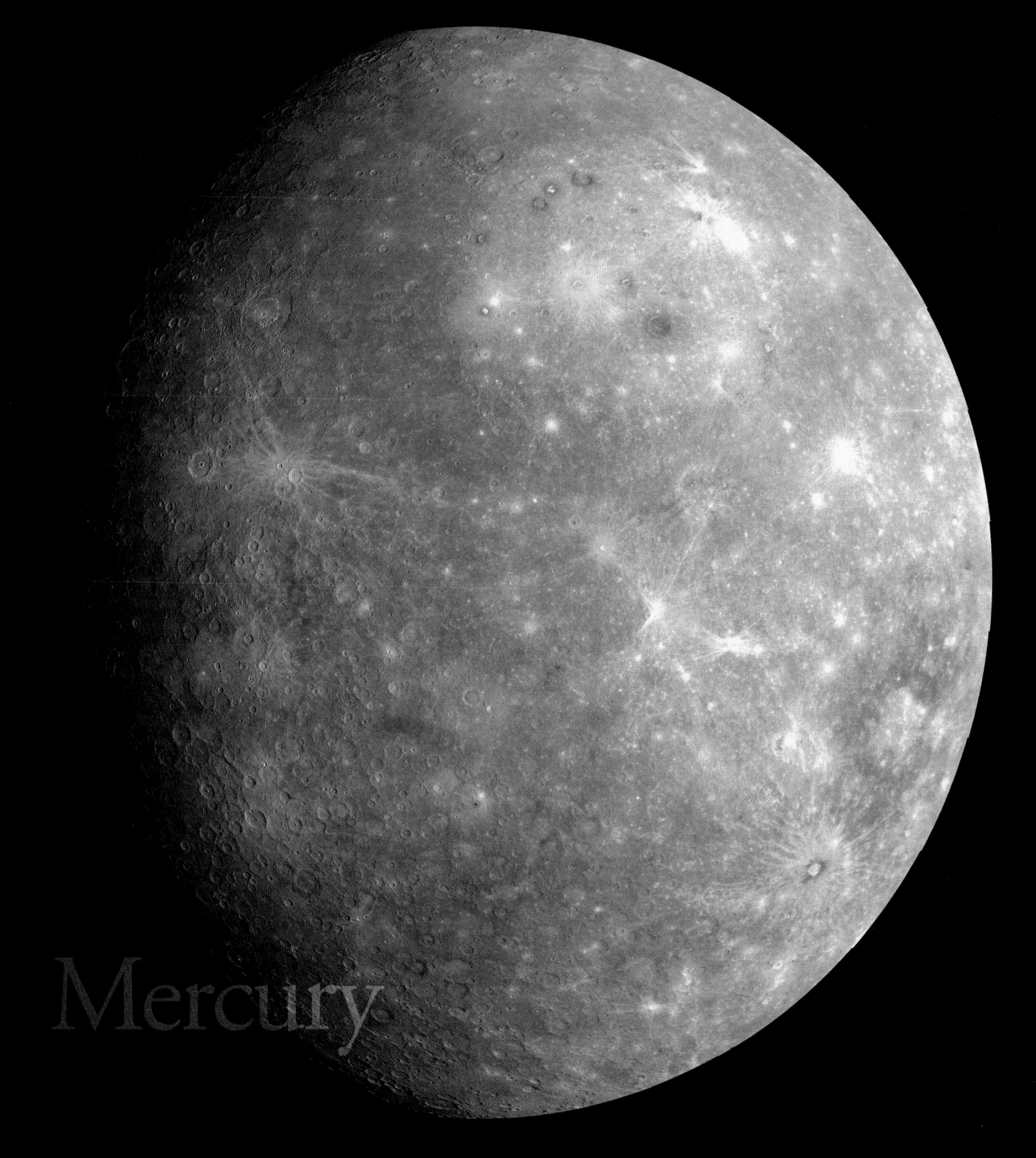

only thing around Mercury that would resemble an atmosphere is a thin **exosphere** made up of atoms blasted off the surface by electrically charged particles from the solar wind and by **micrometeoroid** impacts.[1] These atoms are quickly pushed into space by the intense solar radiation from the nearby sun.

Another unusual fact about Mercury is that its day-night cycle is equivalent to two of its years; in other words, two orbits around the sun. Since one of Mercury's orbits around the sun takes 88 Earth days, the complete day-night cycle on Mercury takes 176 Earth days.[2]

The lack of an atmosphere that could hold heat, combined with Mercury's long, sunless nights, causes the nighttime temperatures on the planet to drop to about -280 degrees Fahrenheit. But at sunrise this all changes as the nearby sun bakes the surface at 800 degrees. Besides this extreme heat, there are also intense magnetic tornados that funnel the hot solar wind plasma and electrically charged particles down to the surface. This blasting of **ions** causes neutrally charged atoms to be knocked out of the ground and hurled high above, eventually becoming lost in space.[3]

Mercury deals with something that we on Earth generally don't have to worry about—the constant bombardment of rocks and boulders from space. The surface of Mercury is pockmarked with hundreds of thousands of craters. The largest one was caused by an asteroid estimated to be roughly 60 miles wide. This rock smashed into the planet and exploded with enormous force. After the debris settled, the damage was visible. A giant hole stretching 960 miles from one end to the other had been blasted into the ground.[4] Named the Caloris Basin, this hole is large enough for the entire state of Texas to fit inside and is a prominent feature of a planet that is only about 3,000 miles in diameter.

Since Mercury is the smallest planet, it also has the lowest gravitational pull. A 150-pound man would weigh 57 pounds on Mercury, and a 70-pound child would weigh only 27 pounds.

The incredible features and fascinating aspects of Mercury are quite literally "out of this world." Yet the Creator finds enjoyment in making and controlling such an otherworldly place. The Bible tells us that all things were created by God for His own pleasure. This includes Mercury.

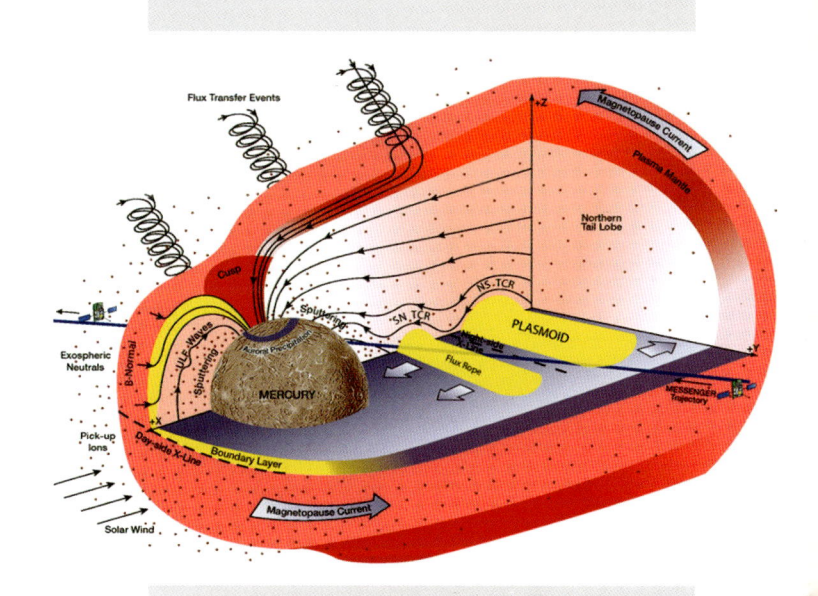

Top: During a flyby in 2008, the MESSENGER spacecraft observed a highly dynamic magnetosphere. This graphic illustrates the intense magnetic tornados that funnel electrically charged solar particles down to the surface of Mercury.

Left: This high-resolution mosaic of images shows Mercury as it appeared to MESSENGER as the spacecraft departed the planet following the mission's first flyby of Mercury. This mosaic shows a portion of the planet never previously seen by spacecraft.

PARADING PLANETS 55

Venus

VENUS – THE MORNING AND EVENING STAR

Venus has been called Earth's "twin sister" because it is almost the same size as Earth and sits next to us in its orbit. Brighter than the stars to the naked eye, Venus is the first beacon to appear in the evening sky when it's in the west, and it is the last light to be extinguished in the morning sky when it's in the east. For this reason, Venus has been called the morning and evening star.

One day on Venus is even longer than its year. While one Venus year lasts 225 Earth days, one of Venus's days is the equivalent of 243 days on Earth.[5]

If we were to take an imaginary journey through space to visit this intriguing planet, we would first be impressed by its balmy appearance. The clouds that cover its surface give Venus an appearance similar to Earth, but many things make this planet radically different from ours. Situated about 26 million miles closer to the sun than Earth, Venus is actually the deadliest planet in our solar system.

Continuing our journey into Venus's atmosphere, the heat would begin to build. Although Mercury is about 31 million miles closer to the sun than Venus, Venus is an average of 500 degrees hotter, making it the hottest of all the planets. This is partly because Venus has a thick atmosphere of mostly carbon dioxide that traps heat from the sun. The atmosphere behaves like a sheet of glass around a greenhouse, letting light and heat in but not allowing heat to escape. The atmosphere is a scorching inferno of hot, dry, acidic air with temperatures around 870 degrees Fahrenheit, making a conventional oven seem like a refrigerator![6]

A shroud of vaporized sulfuric acid clouds completely covers Venus.[7] Below these clouds, an otherworldly sight appears. Through the thick haze of the murky atmosphere, dry plains with thousands of volcanoes come into view. Some of the volcanoes spew lava hundreds of feet into the air and measure up to 150 miles across. Another third of the planet is covered by enormous mountain ranges with peaks reaching up to seven miles high.

On the surface of Venus, broken rocks are strewn across a landscape that has the yellowish color of sulfur. No water exists here, as it has all

Left: This radar image of Venus, taken by the spacecraft Magellan, shows approximately how the surface of the planet appears below the suffocating clouds.

Below: The harsh, acidic atmosphere of Venus is sealed off from above by thick clouds of sulfuric acid that blanket the planet with extreme heat, sulfurous vapors, tremendous air pressure, and powerful lightning strikes. This artist's rendering of the landscape of Venus illustrates the hostile environment.

been boiled away by the heat of the atmosphere. The air itself is so thick and heavy that it crushes down on every square inch of the planet's surface with 1,323 pounds of pressure, the same amount of pressure we would feel if we were 3,000 feet under water.

Trying to survive even a few seconds on Venus would be completely impossible. Any form of life would be crushed, cooked, and corroded almost instantly. Even humans in space suits could not survive the conditions that exist on the surface of Venus. Certain metals could not withstand the heat; lead, for example, would completely melt away. After a few hours, a spacecraft's instruments and functional abilities would be destroyed. The spacecraft best designed to withstand these terrible conditions lasted only 127 minutes before the signal from it was lost. However, it was able to transmit data back to the earth in the short time before it was rendered useless.

Learning about Venus should make us all the more thankful for our planet! God has established a perfect set of checks and balances that make it possible for life to exist on Earth.

MARS – THE RUSTY PLANET

It's a place of enormous dormant volcanoes and gargantuan canyons. Towering dust devils twist wildly across miles and miles of boulder-strewn terrain. High-speed dry winds kick up dust storms that can engulf the entire planet. They whistle and roar as they cut through the rocks and blast down the canyons. Huge impact craters tell of heavy bombardment from the heavens. Temperatures on the planet drop low enough to freeze gases right out of the air into polar ice caps. This is a surreal place of extreme geological features coated with a continuous layer of iron rust and framed by a red sky above. It's a place so far away that its 4,200-mile diameter diminishes into a tiny speck of light when viewed from Earth. This is planet Mars.[8]

Mars is a place where man has never been, yet on its cold, lifeless surface a few alien objects are crawling around, eager to find out more about this fascinating place. These rovers are controlled by

Top: The surface of Venus is continuously covered by thick clouds of sulfuric acid as seen in this photograph.

Middle: On June 5, 2012, Venus drifted silently between the sun and Earth. This rare event is not scheduled to happen again until 2117.

Right: Mars is shown here with the northern polar ice cap prominently displayed. The Valles Marineris canyon system can be seen extending across the lower central portion of the planet. This network of giant ravines is about as wide as the United States.

Mars

A close up view of part of the Valles Marineris canyon system shows brightly layered deposits partially covered by a brown mantle. The photograph shows an approximately ¾-mile section of the canyon system.

people on Earth who drive them around on Mars almost like a boy drives a remote control car. The difference is in the rover's delayed response to the commands given to it. The radio signal that controls the rovers travels at 670 million miles per hour but still takes up to 20 minutes to arrive. Imagine the controller's dilemma when he sees a potentially debilitating boulder immediately ahead, knowing that even if he gives the rover a command to make a right turn, it will continue going straight for 20 minutes.

Mars has been shrouded in mystery, myths, and folklore, a place where many people supposed life could be found. In reality, the planet is more devoid of life than a graveyard. Some men in the nineteenth and early twentieth century claimed to have seen an extensive network of canals cut into the surface of Mars and theorized that they were made by intelligent beings of an advanced civilization. Today we know those were as imaginary as the tooth fairy, optical illusions caused by their poor quality telescopes. After no canals or little green men were found on Mars, many people still hoped to find traces of simple life such as bacteria-like organisms. But these were not found either, so scientists resorted to trying to confirm the existence of water, a basic constituent of life. Frozen water has been found near the polar region of Mars, but life has not been found there or anywhere else in the universe besides Earth. Yet the lore of Mars lives on.

Mars is home to a variety of fascinating geographical features, including an immense system of canyons called Valles Marineris. These supersized gullies run east to west for about 2,500 miles and in some places are about six miles deep, almost five times deeper than the Grand Canyon. The highest known mountain in the solar system exists on Mars; the volcano Olympus Mons towers 17 miles above the surrounding plain. Large impact craters also exist here. Hellas Planitia, the largest of them, is a gigantic hole over five miles deep, with a diameter of about 1,400 miles.

During the Martian winter, temperatures drop low enough to literally freeze air. Carbon dioxide in the atmosphere freezes, forming a coating of what is called dry ice over Mars' polar ice caps. The frozen carbon dioxide then evaporates directly into the atmosphere in springtime. Mars is a fascinating place, but desolation and drought, bombardment and cold, dust and rust reign here, reminding us of what a special oasis God has created on Earth.

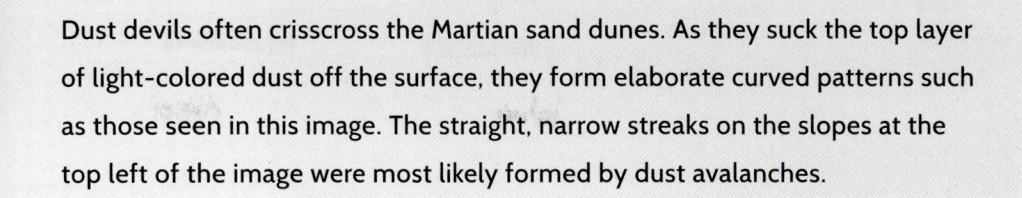

Dust devils often crisscross the Martian sand dunes. As they suck the top layer of light-colored dust off the surface, they form elaborate curved patterns such as those seen in this image. The straight, narrow streaks on the slopes at the top left of the image were most likely formed by dust avalanches.

These strange dark features on the surface of Mars are not easily explained. They may be the result of cold gas jets erupting from below the surface of the planet. As the gas emerges from the surface, it carries dark dust along and scatters it around the area.

This image shows the edge of a dark dune field on the floor of Proctor Crater, one of the many craters on Mars. The dunes are composed of basaltic sand that has collected on the bottom of the crater. Superimposed on their surface are smaller secondary dunes that are commonly seen on terrestrial dunes of this size.

A towering dust devil casts a serpentine shadow over the Martian surface in this image. The image covers an area about four-tenths of a mile (644 meters) across. The length of the dusty whirlwind's shadow indicates that the dust plume reaches more than half a mile in height. The plume is about 30 yards in diameter.

This true-color, simulated view of Jupiter is composed of four images taken by NASA's Cassini spacecraft. These images were combined and projected onto a globe to illustrate what Jupiter would look like if the cameras used to image this planet had a field of view large enough to capture the entire planet. Jupiter's moon Europa is casting the shadow on the planet.

JUPITER – KING OF THE PLANETS

Jupiter, the goliath of our solar system, is the largest planet, measuring approximately 88,846 miles across. This is about 11 times the diameter of Earth. Jupiter is bigger and heavier than all the other planets combined, yet it shows up as only a pinpoint of light in the night sky because it is so far away from Earth. If Jupiter were as close to us as the moon, it would appear much larger, stretching over 40 times farther across the sky than the moon does.

Although Jupiter is so large, it actually rotates faster than Earth, taking 9 hours and 56 minutes to spin once, compared to 24 hours for Earth.[9] The rotation speed at Jupiter's equator is over 25,000 miles per hour compared to Earth's speed of 1,000 miles per hour. This high rate of rotation causes Jupiter to flatten out somewhat at the poles and bulge at the equator. The distance from the eastern side of Jupiter to its western side is over 5,000 miles more than the distance between its northern and southern poles.

Jupiter's size produces enormous gravitational attraction. At its surface, Jupiter's gravity is about 2½ times that of Earth's. This means that a person who weighs 100 pounds on Earth would weigh about 253 pounds on Jupiter. Jupiter actually helps protect Earth from bombardment by swallowing up asteroids and comets that could potentially collide with it.

In 1992, a comet (Shoemaker-Levy 9) passed too closely to Jupiter and was broken into pieces by the tidal forces of its strong gravitational pull. Scientists estimated that the largest pieces were up to 2½ miles in diameter. Then, in July of 1994, when the comet passed by again, the fragments were captured by the planet's gravity and were hurled into Jupiter. This impact caused powerful explosions that scattered comet debris over areas as large as the Earth's diameter.[10]

Another feature not to be missed on Jupiter is an enor-

The comet that was broken up by Jupiter's pull stretched into a train of 21 icy fragments spread across 710,000 miles of space—three times the distance between Earth and the moon. This photograph of the fragments was taken two months before they collided with Jupiter.

The largest storm in the solar system rages on after hundreds of years, churning at speeds of up to 300 miles per hour. The Great Red Spot covers an area much larger than Earth itself.

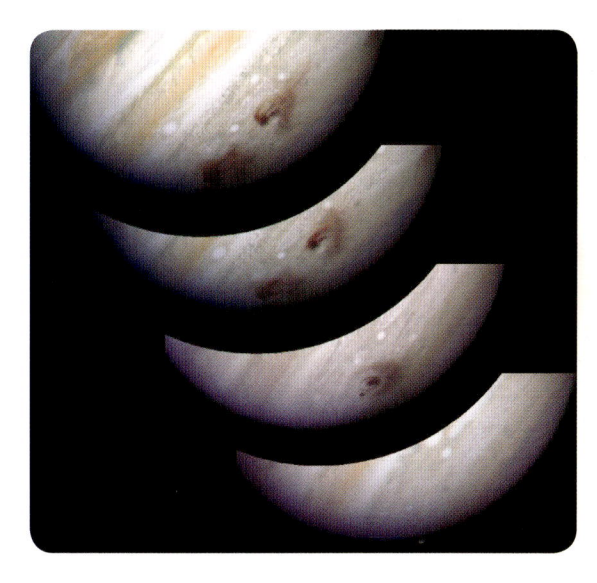

A series of photographs show the aftereffects of the comet Shoemaker-Levy 9. The bottom image shows the impact plume erupting off the planet about five minutes after the collision. The last image at the top was taken five days later.

PARADING PLANETS **63**

mous storm named the Great Red Spot. On Earth, hurricanes can form and dissipate in a matter of days, but on Jupiter they can last for centuries. This storm resembles a large hurricane and was discovered in the late 1600s. It varies in size, but currently the diameter of the spot at its widest place is close to three times that of Earth. The outer edge of the storm circulates at about 225 miles per hour. It is believed that the storm routinely kicks up wind gusts of over 300 miles per hour.

Jupiter has more satellites or moons than any other planet; at least 63 moons orbit it. Four of these moons can easily be seen through a small telescope or even some binoculars. These four moons are all at least 1,900 miles in diameter, making them larger than the dwarf planet Pluto. Most of the 59 remaining moons are less than five miles across. Each one of them has widely varying compositions, chemicals, and geographical features, but none of them are as special, or uniquely suited for life, as Earth.

SATURN – THE RINGED PLANET

Saturn, with its halo of rings made of shimmering ice particles, is doubtless one of God's most unique and beautiful creations. Saturn is extremely large for a planet; so large, in fact, that you could place 9 Earths across its face, or pour in over 700 of them to fill it up. Although it is so large, it is fairly light in comparison to the other planets. Its density is only about two-thirds that of water.

Looking through a backyard telescope, a person will notice that

While cruising around Saturn in early October 2004, Cassini captured a series of images that have been composed into this large, global, natural-color view of Saturn and its rings. This grand mosaic consists of 126 images acquired in a tile-like fashion, covering one end of Saturn's rings to the other and the entire planet in between.

If you want to see a picture painted as only the hand of God can paint, GO WITH ME TO SATURN.
JOHN H. THAYER

Saturn

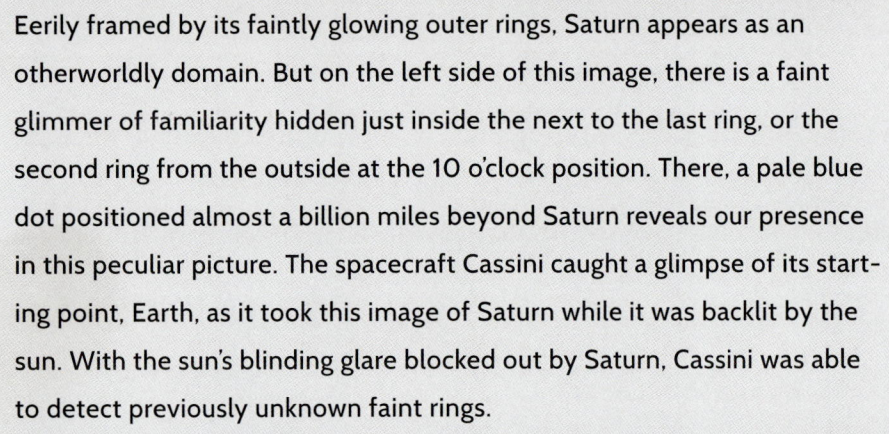

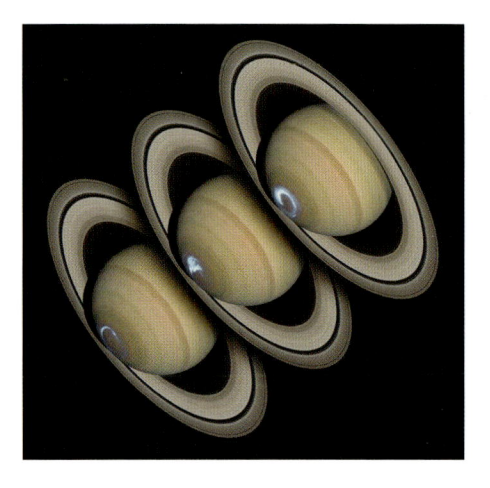

Eerily framed by its faintly glowing outer rings, Saturn appears as an otherworldly domain. But on the left side of this image, there is a faint glimmer of familiarity hidden just inside the next to the last ring, or the second ring from the outside at the 10 o'clock position. There, a pale blue dot positioned almost a billion miles beyond Saturn reveals our presence in this peculiar picture. The spacecraft Cassini caught a glimpse of its starting point, Earth, as it took this image of Saturn while it was backlit by the sun. With the sun's blinding glare blocked out by Saturn, Cassini was able to detect previously unknown faint rings.

The dancing light of an aurora circles Saturn's polar region, testifying to the sun's far-reaching effect on a planet that is over nine times farther from the sun than Earth is.

This cross section of Saturn's rings shows their detailed structure.

Colombo Gap
Maxwell Gap

D Ring
74,500 km
C Ring
92,000 km
B R

This dramatic view of Saturn shows the rings nearly straight-on, while the shadows of the rings are unfurled across the northern regions of the planet. The imposing presence of Saturn's icy moon Dione hovers in the foreground.

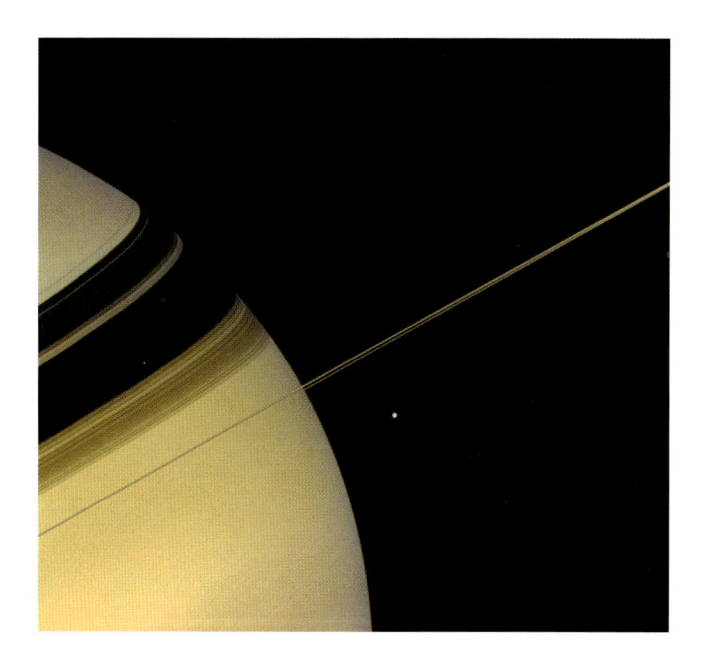

The serene beauty of Saturn invites the Cassini spacecraft's gaze as the spacecraft hurtles through this dynamic system, studying the giant planet's rings, moons, atmosphere, and magnetosphere. The icy moon Mimas to the right of the planet is about 112,000 miles closer to Cassini than Saturn in this scene.

Huygens Gap | Encke Gap | Keeler Gap

117,580 km | Cassini Division | 122,200 km | A Ring | 136,780 km | F Ring | 140,220 km

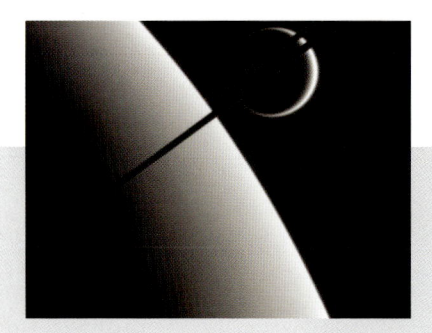

Above: Saturn and its ring system loom in the foreground, while its largest moon Titan appears as a slender crescent in the distance.

Top left: This ringside view captures four of Saturn's moons in one image. Saturn lies outside of this image to the left, but the outer regions of its rings are shown on this picture. The largest moon, Titan, is in the background. At 3,200 miles in diameter, it is about 50 percent larger than Earth's moon. In front of Titan, Dione appears to be hovering above the rings. It is smaller at 698 miles in diameter. To the right of the rings is the small moon Pandora. It measures only 50 miles across. And finally, the tiny moon Pan sits nestled in the gap in the rings on the left side of the image. At only 17 miles across, Pan is about the size of a large city.

Middle: This bizarre scene shows the cloud-streaked side of Saturn in front of one of the planet's rings. The ring's image is warped near the planet by the gas in Saturn's upper atmosphere.

Bottom: The huge storm churning through the atmosphere in Saturn's northern hemisphere overtakes itself as it encircles the planet in this true-color view from NASA's Cassini spacecraft. This picture, captured on February 25, 2011, was taken about 12 weeks after the storm began, and by this time the clouds had formed a tail that wrapped around the planet.

the rings around Saturn appear to be a solid disk. In reality, they are made up of many individual particles held in place by gravity and orbiting the planet in an endless marathon. The particles normally range in size from a grain of salt to a large rock, but some of them can be as large as a house. They are mostly made of ice or bits of rocks coated with ice. Some gaps are visible in the rings; these are caused by small moons whose gravity pulls ice particles away from the rings. These moons also move through the gaps as they orbit Saturn. Saturn's rings have a diameter of more than 150,000 miles and a typical thickness of only about 30 feet, although in some areas the particles pile up into mounds over two miles high. Nonetheless, the rings appear extremely thin when viewed from Earth. In fact, if they are tilted with the edge directly toward us, the rings are not visible at all.[11]

Saturn is the farthest planet from Earth that can be seen with the naked eye. Because of its distance from the sun, it doesn't get as much heat as Earth does, but the pressure in its core causes the planet to heat itself. It creates more heat from the pressure than it receives from the sun.[12]

Saturn rotates at over 20,000 miles per hour at the equator. This speed makes it flatten at the poles more than any other planet. This effect is easy to see through a small telescope. The distance from the eastern to the western side of Saturn is about 10 percent greater than the distance from the north to the south.

Astronomers have discovered that there are at least 62 moons orbiting Saturn.[13] This planet with its halo of shining ice and abundance of circling moons is another reminder of the glory and creative ability of God.

URANUS & NEPTUNE – GAS GIANT TWINS

Two enormous orbs of gas, liquid, and ice, orbiting the sun at the far edge of our solar system, dwarf the earth in size

The planet Uranus hangs suspended in the inky blackness of space as seen by the spacecraft Voyager 2 in 1986.

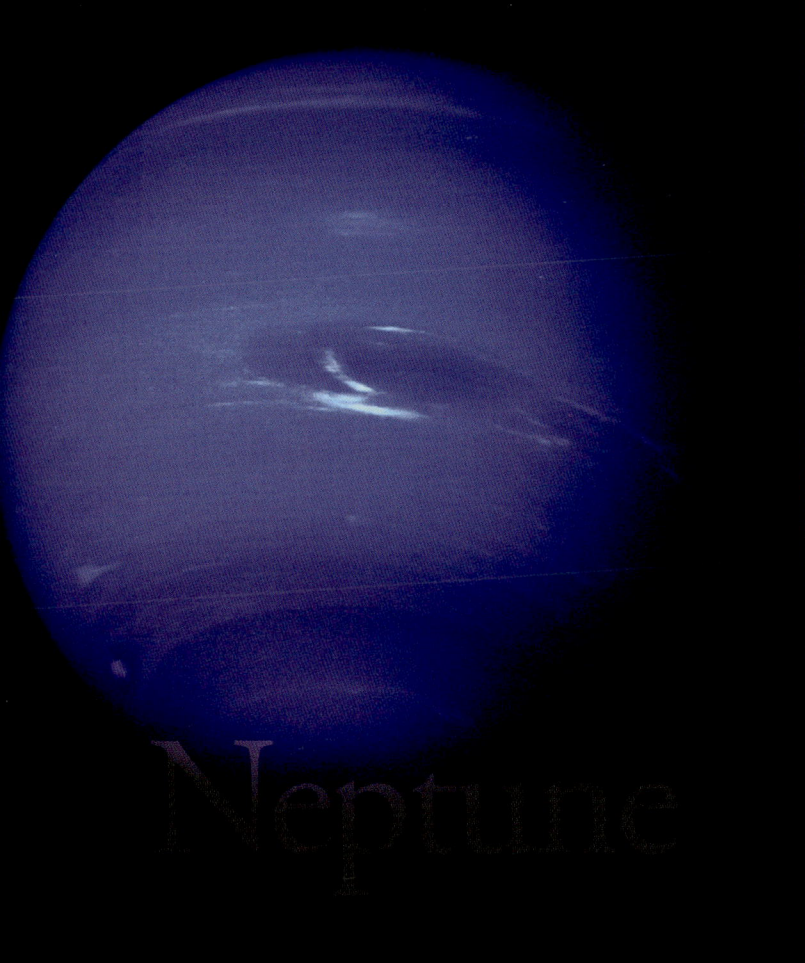

This picture of Neptune shows the storm named the Great Dark Spot as it appeared in 1998. Neptune has the fastest winds in our solar system.

This image from Voyager 2 clearly shows vertical height in the fast-moving clouds above Neptune.

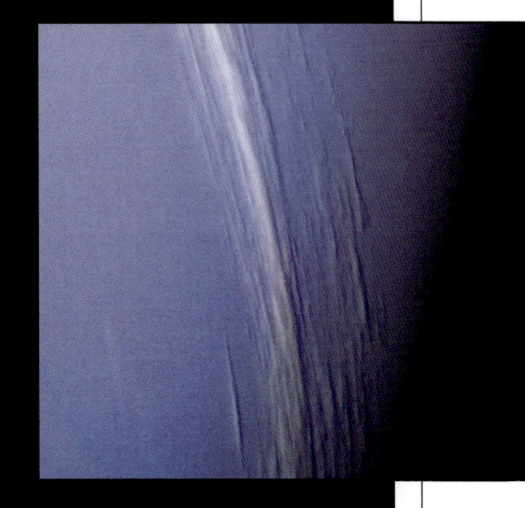

and weight. In fact, the combined mass of these two planets is over 30 times greater than Earth's. Astronomers calculate the weight of Uranus to be 95 sextillion tons. Neptune is about 20 percent heavier than Uranus.

Uranus, which was discovered first and is the closer of the two, is the coldest planet in the solar system with a temperature of -357 degrees Fahrenheit. The core of the planet is warmer, however, due to intense pressure. This means that not all of Uranus is frozen. Most of the mass of Uranus resides in a liquid core made up of partially frozen water, methane, and ammonia. The blue-green color of Uranus is a result of the methane gas in its atmosphere.

If we were to stand on the ammonia and methane ice floes of Uranus's surface, we could look up and see its 27 moons silently circling the planet against a backdrop of thousands of stars. From the horizon, the soft, silver glow of nine inner rings extends upward, stretching across the sky. Glowing above those are the colored outer rings, one blue and another red.[14]

The nearly perpendicular axis of Uranus presents a dilemma for the evolutionary theory of origins of the solar system. According to the theory, the solar system began as a rotating proto-planetary disk of dust. This dust then began to coalesce into the sun and planets. If this were actually the case, all the planets should have vertical axes as they spin like tops in their orbits. But Uranus is tipped over on its side and practically rolls around its orbit instead of spinning like the other planets. And spinning planets can't simply fall over; they are like gyroscopes with locked orientations. Venus also poses a problem for this theory. Depending on how you look at it, Venus would have had to turn completely upside down after its counter-clockwise motion began, or it would have started out spinning a completely opposite direction from the rest of the

chapter four
Galaxies: Island Universes

Who of us has not gone out and looked up into the night sky, only to be overwhelmed at the thousands of stars that twinkle from every corner? Their silent message is so profound that it can practically deafen our senses and numb our intellect. The tiny portion of the heavens that we see proficiently declares the glory of God, but beyond that portion lies so much more that is hidden from view.

Stars are not just scattered in random locations across the universe. Rather, they are grouped together into enormous "island universes" called galaxies. The groups are so large that telescopes are needed just to look past our group and view the stars in others.

When we put the telescopes away and look up into the night sky with unaided eyes, we can see only a tiny corner of our home galaxy called the Milky Way. In fact, the area we are looking into while seeing individual stars is only about one-twentieth the diameter of the Milky Way. Even if we could see the complete galaxy, it is only a miniscule part of a universe whose boundaries have yet to be found.

On a clear night, the Milky Way Galaxy appears as a milky glow that stretches from the southern horizon to the northern horizon. The milky glow comes from the combined light of millions of stars too far away to be seen with the naked eye. The band of light we see is only one of the spiral arms of the galaxy. Following the band toward the south directs us toward the center of the Milky Way.

The Milky Way measures about 100,000 light-years across, or over 587 million billion miles! It contains at least 100 billion stars. Although the Milky Way is such an enormous galaxy, it is really just a speck of dust in a countless sea of galaxies that stretch across the cosmos. Astronomers have found so many galaxies that it is simply impossible to count them all. In fact, for every one of the stars in our galaxy, there is at least another entire galaxy of millions and billions of stars somewhere in the universe. These stars hold such a great amount of potential energy that if one of them would burst into a supernova explosion, it would briefly outshine the entire galaxy of billions of stars that it's in.

Ah Lord GOD! behold, thou hast made the heaven and the earth **by thy great power and stretched out arm, and there is nothing too hard for thee.**

JEREMIAH 32:17

Hoag's Object

A nearly perfect ring of blue stars pinwheels about the yellow nucleus of an unusual galaxy known as Hoag's Object. This image from NASA's Hubble Space Telescope captures a face-on view of the galaxy's ring of stars, revealing more detail than any other existing photo of this object.

The entire galaxy is about 120,000 light-years wide, which is slightly larger than our Milky Way Galaxy. Curiously, an object that bears an uncanny resemblance to Hoag's Object can be seen in the gap at the 1 o'clock position. The object appears to be a background galaxy like Hoag's Object.

NGC 5584

The brilliant blue glow of young stars traces the graceful spiral arms of Galaxy NGC 5584 in this Hubble Space Telescope image. Thin, dark dust lanes appear to be flowing from the yellowish core, where older stars reside. The reddish dots sprinkled throughout the image are largely background galaxies. NGC 5584 resides 72 million light-years away from Earth in the direction of the constellation Virgo.

M81

M81 is one of the brightest galaxies that can be seen from Earth. It is high in the northern sky in the direction of the circumpolar constellation Ursa Major, or the Great Bear, and is just at the limit of naked-eye visibility. From Earth, it appears to be about the same size as the full moon. Though the galaxy is located 11.6 million light-years away, the Hubble Space Telescope's view is so sharp that it can identify individual stars, along with open star clusters, globular star clusters, and even glowing regions of fluorescent gas.

Located 12 million light-years away, M82 appears high in the northern spring sky in the direction of the constellation Ursa Major, the Great Bear. The galaxy is remarkable for its bright blue disk, webs of shredded clouds, and fiery-looking plumes of glowing hydrogen blasting out of its central regions. In M82, young stars are crammed into tiny but massive star clusters. These, in turn, congregate by the dozens to make the bright patches, or "starburst clumps," in the central parts of M82. The clusters in the clumps can be distinguished only in the sharp Hubble images. Most of the pale, white objects sprinkled around the body of M82 that look like fuzzy stars are actually individual star clusters about 20 light-years across that contain up to a million stars.

M82

GALAXIES: ISLAND UNIVERSES   77

NGC 634

This spiral galaxy, NGC 634, was discovered in the nineteenth century by French astronomer Édouard Jean-Marie Stephan, but in 2008 it became a prime target for observations thanks to the violent demise of a white dwarf star. This supernova, known as SN2008a, was spotted in the galaxy and briefly rivaled the brilliance of its entire host galaxy. Despite the energy of the explosion, SN2008a can no longer be seen in this Hubble image, which was taken around a year and a half later.

THE CELESTIAL MESSAGE

Parallels and Lessons from the Solar System

The **SUN** gives light and life.

The **SUN** is the center of the solar system.

The **PLANETS** revolve around the sun.

The **MOON** reflects sunlight to lighten the night.

The **SON** gives spiritual light and life.

The **SON** is the center of the kingdom.

The lives of **GOD'S PEOPLE** revolve around the Son.

GOD'S PEOPLE reflect Son-light to lighten this dark world.

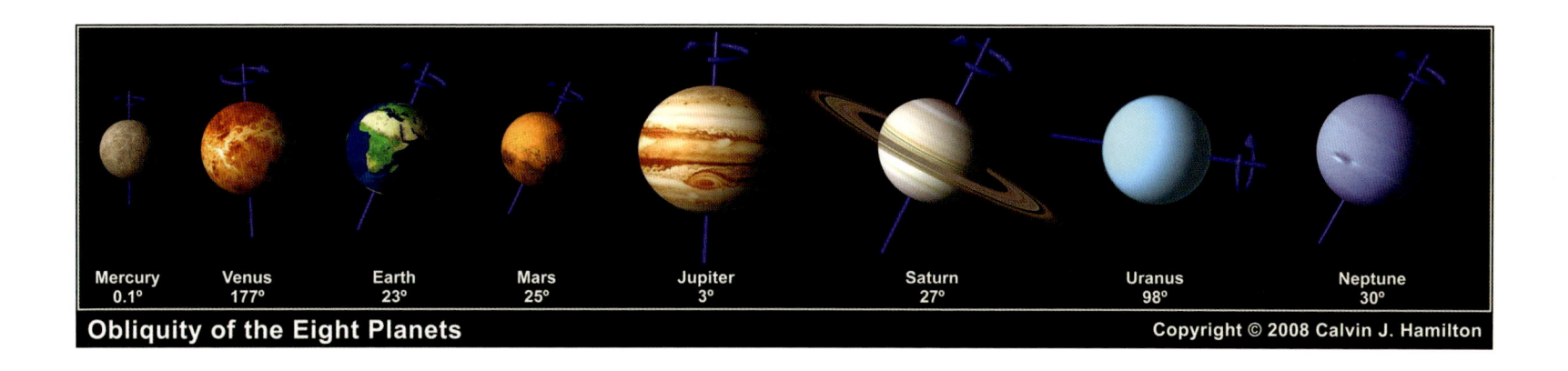

Obliquity of the Eight Planets

Mercury 0.1° | Venus 177° | Earth 23° | Mars 25° | Jupiter 3° | Saturn 27° | Uranus 98° | Neptune 30°

Copyright © 2008 Calvin J. Hamilton

solar system. Neither one of these scenarios is likely.

After the discovery of Uranus in 1781, some astronomers noticed its orbit had a few unexplained irregularities. John Couch Adams, a mathematician in England, performed an investigation to determine what caused this. Adams had an extraordinary ability to do mathematical calculations in his head, even when he was a very young boy. He studied irregularities in the orbit of Uranus and theorized that the irregular orbit of Uranus was caused by another planet farther out in the solar system. He had mentally worked out all the orbital calculations in his head without using pen and paper. Another Frenchman named Le Verrier calculated the existence of another planet as well. Shortly after this, the other planet was found and named Neptune. It was the first planet discovered by mathematical calculations.

Neptune is the windiest planet in the solar system with winds up to 1,500 miles per hour. Winds of this speed were measured in a storm called the Great Dark Spot. The Voyager 2 spacecraft tracked this enormous dark storm, the size of planet Earth, rotating like a hurricane and charging west across Neptune at 750 miles per hour.[15]

Neptune is such a long way from the sun that it takes 165 Earth years for Neptune to make one orbit around the sun. 2011 marked the first time that Neptune had completed one full year, or orbit, since it was discovered in 1846.

Neptune has a large moon named Triton. It is one of the coldest places in the solar system, even colder than the planet Uranus, with temperatures dipping to -391 degrees Fahrenheit. However, Voyager 2 detected geysers on Triton spewing ice more than five miles into the air, indicating that the interior of the moon is warm.[16]

The planets, with their unique characteristics and diverse features, are truly remarkable. With only a word spoken from the mouth of God, they appeared from nowhere in their perfect state.

For all the gods of the people are idols:

BUT THE LORD MADE THE HEAVENS.

1 CHRONICLES 16:26

Messier 74

Messier 74, located roughly 32 million light-years away, is a stunning example of a "grand-design" spiral galaxy that is viewed by Earth observers nearly face-on. Its perfectly symmetrical spiral arms emanate from the central nucleus and are dotted with clusters of blue stars and glowing pink regions of ionized hydrogen. Tracing along the spiral arms are winding dust lanes that also begin very near the galaxy's nucleus and follow along the length of the arms.

NGC 1275

This Hubble Space Telescope image of galaxy NGC 1275 reveals the fine, thread-like filamentary structures in the gas surrounding the galaxy. The red filaments are composed of cool gas being suspended by a magnetic field and are surrounded by the hot gas (100 million degrees Fahrenheit) in the center of the Perseus galaxy cluster.

GALAXIES: ISLAND UNIVERSES

NGC 1300

The Hubble telescope captured a spectacle of starlight, glowing gas, and silhouetted dark clouds of interstellar dust in this photograph of the barred spiral galaxy NGC 1300. The spiral arms are gravitationally connected to a straight central bar of stars that crosses the center. The glow that can be seen across the galaxy and especially in the core is the combined light of millions of stars. Distant galaxies can be seen scattered across the background of this image.

THE CELESTIAL MESSAGE

NGC 1316

Like dust bunnies that lurk in corners and hide under beds, surprisingly complex loops and blobs of cosmic dust lie hidden in the giant elliptical galaxy NGC 1316.

GALAXIES: ISLAND UNIVERSES

NGC 2841

An imposing, majestic disk of stars interwoven with dust lanes is visible here in this close-up view of spiral galaxy NGC 2841. This massive galaxy is over 150,000 light-years across, considerably larger than our own Milky Way Galaxy.

NGC 7049

This striking image of NGC 7049 shows a lacy web of dust lanes dramatically backlit by the combined glow of millions of stars in the halo of the galaxy. This mysterious and delightful galaxy resembles a freshly stirred mug of hot chocolate.

GALAXIES: ISLAND UNIVERSES

Sombrero Galaxy

NASA's Hubble Space Telescope has trained its razor-sharp eye on one of the universe's most stately and photogenic galaxies, the Sombrero Galaxy, or Messier 104 (M104). The galaxy's hallmark is a brilliant white, bulbous core encircled by the thick dust lanes comprising the spiral structure of the galaxy. From Earth, we view the galaxy just six degrees north of its equatorial plane. It appears tilted and its edge faces us. This brilliant galaxy was named the Sombrero because of its resemblance to the broad-rimmed, high-topped Mexican hat.

M104 is just beyond the limit of naked-eye visibility and is easily seen through small telescopes. It lies at the southern edge of the rich Virgo cluster of galaxies and is one of the most massive objects in that group, equivalent to 800 billion suns.

The Mice

These two galaxies, nicknamed The Mice, are seen after they have passed through each other once and as they are getting ready to pass through each other again. When one galaxy passes through another, rarely do the stars in them actually collide. There is enough empty space between the stars that the galaxies can sail directly through each other with little consequence other than the massive gravitational disturbance that can scatter and relocate stars across thousands of light-years of space.

The larger the sea of knowledge, **the greater the boundaries of the unknown.**

I can see how it might be possible for a man to look down upon the earth and be an atheist, **but I cannot conceive how he could look up into the heavens and say there is no God.**

ABRAHAM LINCOLN

Tadpole Galaxy

Against a stunning backdrop of thousands of galaxies, this odd-looking galaxy with a long streamer of stars appears to be racing through space like a runaway pinwheel. Dubbed the Tadpole, this spiral galaxy is unlike the textbook images of stately galaxies. Its distorted shape was caused by a small interloper, a very blue, compact galaxy visible in the upper left corner of the more massive Tadpole. Seen shining through the Tadpole's disk, the tiny intruder is likely a hit-and-run galaxy that is now leaving the scene of the accident. Strong gravitational forces from the interaction created the long tail of debris, consisting of stars and gas that stretch out more than 280,000 light-years. The galactic carnage is playing out against a spectacular backdrop: a "wallpaper pattern" of 6,000 galaxies.

When I consider thy heavens, the work of thy fingers, the moon and the stars, which thou hast ordained; WHAT IS MAN, THAT THOU ART MINDFUL OF HIM? AND THE SON OF MAN, THAT THOU VISITEST HIM?

PSALM 8:3–4

The Rose

In this stunning image, we see how the Creator formed these twisting galaxies to strikingly resemble a beautiful rose. This especially photogenic group of interacting galaxies was photographed in celebration of Hubble's twenty-first anniversary.

THE CELESTIAL MESSAGE

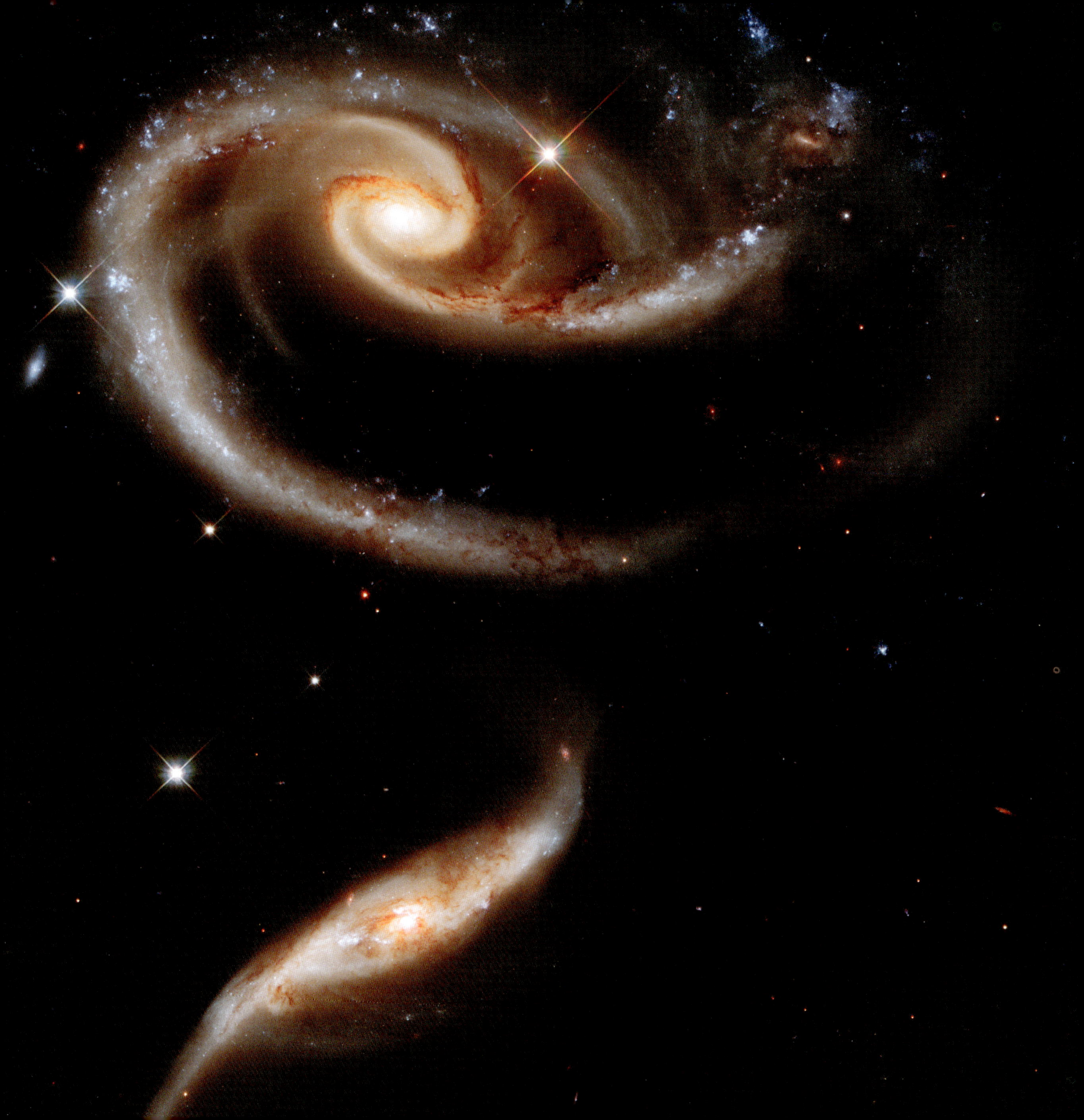

Because God is STRONG, His creation shows *power;*

Because God is GREAT, His creation is *vast;*

Because God is BEAUTIFUL, His creation reflects *glory;*

Because God is LOVE, His creation includes *you.*

The Hubble Ultra Deep Field photograph at right may be one of the most misleading images from the Hubble Space Telescope. At first glance, we seem to see galaxies by the thousands spread through this image, giving the false impression that we are looking across a wide segment of the universe. In reality, we are looking at an area of the sky so small it could easily be hidden behind the twinkling glare of a bright star. God's Word says that the number of stars in the sky is comparable to the number of grains of sand on the seashore. This is hard to imagine at first. It becomes more believable, however, when we realize that a single speck of sand, held at arm's length, could completely blot out the entire section of sky pictured on this Hubble Ultra Deep Field photograph.[1] Behind the area covered by that single grain of sand lie almost 10,000 galaxies. In every one of those galaxies reside a host of stars, about 100 billion on average. Many of those stars are circled by beautiful halos of colorful stellar material in the form of planetary nebulae. Others hold planets and asteroids in their gravitational grasp. Even though it stretches the imagination, it is not illogical to conclude that there could be about one quadrillion stars behind that speck of dirt. How many sand grains would it take to cover the entire night sky? How much is there to see that will never be seen? The whole sky contains 12.7 million times more area than this photograph.[2]

When this picture was taken, astronomers were looking so far out in the universe that light from the most distant galaxies trickled onto the camera's sensors at the rate of about one photon (light particle) per minute. Because of this, the total exposure time had to be 275 hours long. If the entire sky were surveyed in this manner it would take almost one million years of uninterrupted observing.[3]

Every smudge of light on the image is an entire galaxy, containing millions and billions of stars. Only the points of light with four symmetrical diffraction spikes are stars in our own Milky Way Galaxy.[4]

To get this image, Hubble did not have to find a special place in the sky that was crowded. In fact, views of this patch of sky from smaller ground-based telescopes show a basically empty area. This area was deliberately chosen so that nothing would obstruct Hubble's view of deep space.

Hubble Ultra Deep Field

Galaxies, galaxies everywhere, as far as NASA's Hubble Space Telescope can see. This view of nearly 10,000 galaxies is the deepest visible-light image of the cosmos. Called the Hubble Ultra Deep Field, this galaxy-studded view represents a "deep" core sample of the universe, extending out to approximately 13.2 billion light-years.

Orion Nebula

chapter five
Nebulae: Veils of Glory

Tonight's forecast for space is, as always, partly cloudy. Although you may not always see clouds in our atmosphere when you look at the sky, if you look up into the stars with a telescope, you can always see clouds scattered around. These cosmic clouds are called nebulae. The term nebula comes from the Latin word for cloud. Nebulae are enormous and are much larger than Earth itself. Many of these clouds are larger than even our solar system. They are made of gas and dust particles that hang suspended in space. The gas and dust in these clouds are continuously billowing through space, carried about by the powerful radiation from nearby stars. Yet from our perspective, they don't appear to be continuously changing like the clouds on Earth since they are so large and far away from us. The large nebulae maintain their general appearance even though the dust is being pushed thousands of miles across space.

REFLECTION AND EMISSION NEBULAE

Reflection nebulae are clouds of gas and dust in space that shine by reflecting starlight from the stars scattered around them. Emission nebulae emit their own light when radiation from nearby stars excite the gas in the nebulae, causing it to glow. If a nebula is not close enough to the stars around it, it will neither reflect nor emit light and is called a dark nebula.

The Orion Nebula, in the sword of the constellation Orion, is an example of an emission nebula. It is one of the most extraordinary and beautiful objects we can see in the sky, created simply to bring glory to its Creator.

This dramatic image offers a peek inside a cavern of roiling dust and gas. The image represents the sharpest view ever taken of this region, called the Orion Nebula. More than 3,000 stars of various sizes appear in this image. Some of them have never been seen in visible light. These stars reside in a dramatic dust-and-gas landscape of plateaus, mountains, and valleys that are reminiscent of the Grand Canyon.

Astronomers used 520 Hubble images, taken in five colors, to make this picture. They also added ground-based photos to fill out the nebula. Even though the nebula is about 30 billion times farther away from us than the moon, its immense diameter of 24 light-years causes it to cover approximately the same amount of area in our view of the sky as the full moon.

LOOK

Eagle Nebula

From a distance, this cloud named the Eagle Nebula somewhat resembles an eagle with its wings spread in flight. Up close, however, we see a huge cavity surrounded by interstellar gas and dust. In the heart of the cavity are several columns of dust that have been nicknamed the Pillars of Creation. Though the nebula lies about 6,500 light-years away, it can still be seen with a simple pair of binoculars. This testifies to its incredible size. Yet there are other nebulae that dwarf it. One example is the Carina Nebula; it stretches out over 10 times the diameter of the Eagle Nebula.

CLOSER

Here a close-up photograph shows three pillars rising into the open cavity in the heart of the Eagle Nebula. The pillar on the left is four light-years from top to bottom. It's a distance so great that the human mind can scarcely comprehend it. If we could place the earth next to this pillar at the proper scale, it would be completely invisible. The sun is so large, it could be filled with over one million Earths, but even if a circle the size of the sun were on this picture, it could not be seen. In fact, it would take over 27 million suns stacked on top of each other to reach from the bottom to the top of the pillar. Finally, since neither the earth nor the sun is adequate to compare with this colossal giant, we'll compare it to the solar system—over five billion miles from one end to the other and 6,000 times larger than the sun's diameter. A ring representing the solar system on this image would be smaller than one-third of a pixel, and the resolution of this picture would still not be good enough to properly show it! Yet, these pillars are only a small part of the entire nebula. If God's simple dust is so utterly incomprehensible, how much more inconceivable is He? Understandably He asks the question, "To whom then will ye liken me?"

THE CELESTIAL MESSAGE

To whom then will ye liken God?
OR WHAT LIKENESS WILL YE COMPARE UNTO HIM?
ISAIAH 40:18

That an eternal being so exceedingly powerful can be moved into action by the transient thought of one's prayerful heart is **utterly astounding.**

NEBULAE: VEILS OF GLORY

Pillar in the Eagle

This is a billowing tower of cold gas and dust rising from the Eagle Nebula. The soaring tower is 9.5 light-years or about 57 trillion miles high, about twice the distance from our sun to the next nearest star. The starlight is responsible for illuminating the tower's rough surface. Ghostly streamers of gas can be seen boiling off this surface, creating the haze around the structure and highlighting its three-dimensional shape.

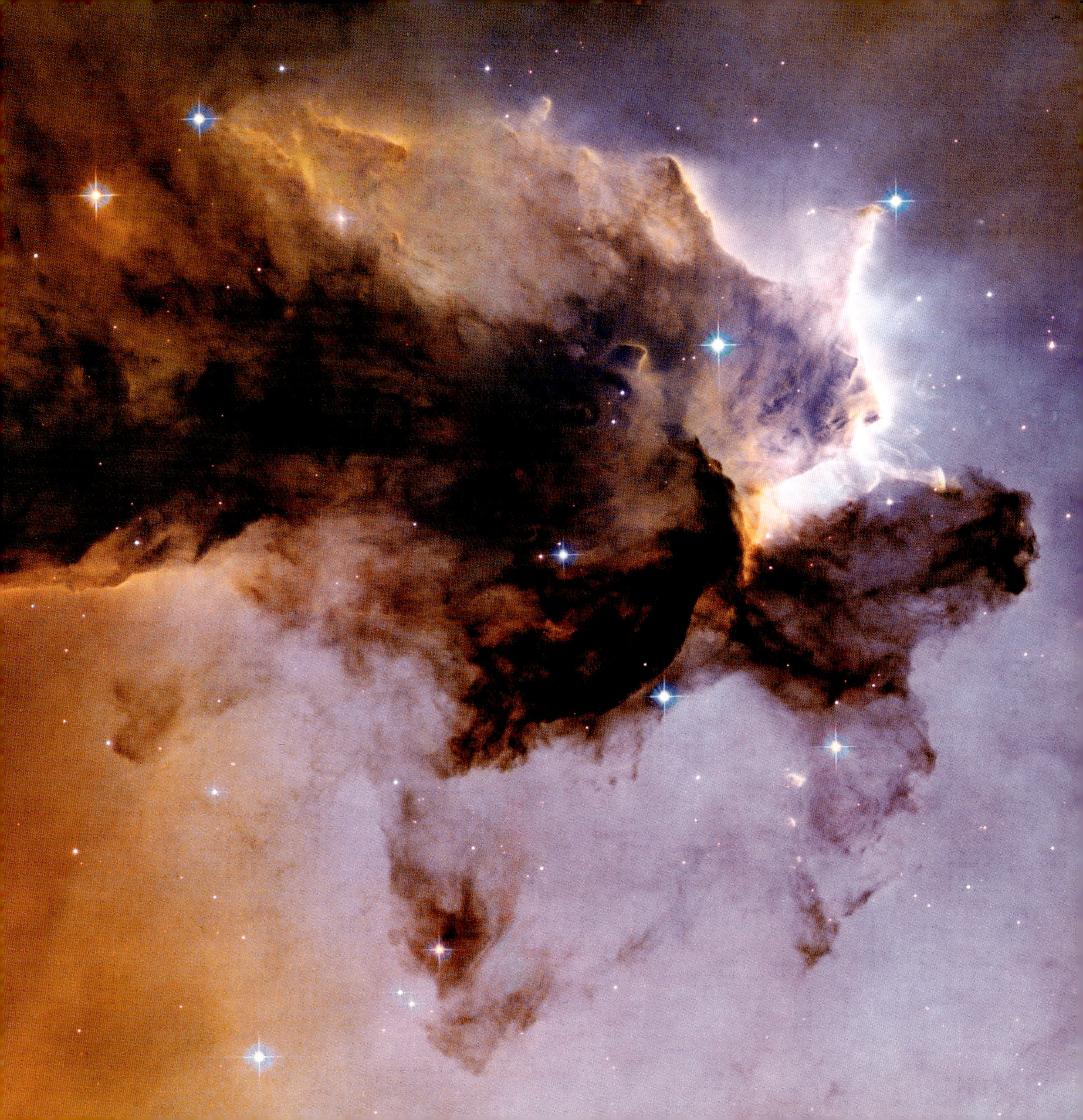

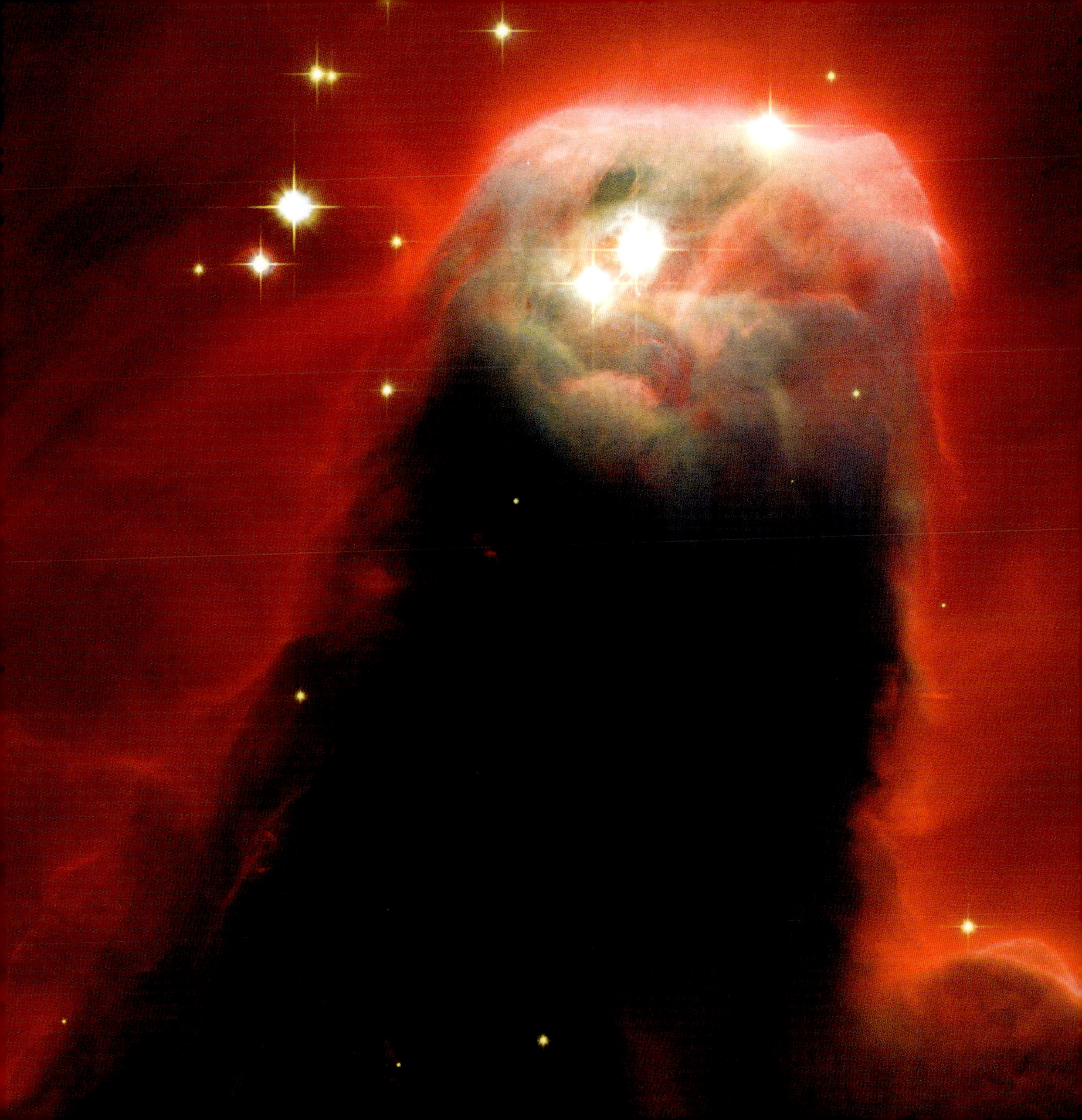

THE HUMAN SOUL CAN SEEM INEXTRICABLY BOUND BY THE PHYSICAL REALM OF THE EARTH AND UTTERLY DETACHED FROM THE SPIRITUAL REALITY OF GOD, *but take a walk with the Lord under the expanse of glory in the glittering heavens and watch as your spirit is quickened, your prayers are invigorated, and your heart soars beyond the stars.*

Cone Nebula

Resembling a nightmarish beast rearing its head from a crimson sea, this monstrous object is actually an innocuous pillar of gas and dust. It's called the Cone Nebula because of its conical shape. This picture shows the upper 2.5 light-years of the nebula, a height that equals 23 million round trips to the moon. The entire nebula is seven light-years long. The Cone Nebula resides 2,500 light-years away in the constellation Monoceros.

Carina Nebula

One of the largest panoramic images ever taken by Hubble is shown here. Forty-eight photographs were combined to make this one high resolution image. The Carina Nebula is an estimated 7,500 light-years from Earth. As one of the largest nebulae ever found, it spans an estimated 200 light-years. To fit the nebula in the empty space between the sun and the next nearest star, it would have to be folded over 45 times. The image here is a portion of the nebula, only 50 light-years wide. That's still more than three million times the distance from the earth to the sun.

Lagoon Nebula

A part of the Lagoon Nebula stretches across this image, showcasing its surreal backdrop of thick interstellar gas. High energy stars dump enormous amounts of ultraviolet radiation through the nebula, causing the gas to ionize and glow colorfully, similar to neon lights. Although the nebula is over 4,000 light-years away, it is large enough and bright enough to be faintly seen with the naked eye as a colorless patch of haze.

Inset: Giant sheets of dust hang suspended in space in this view of part of the Lagoon Nebula

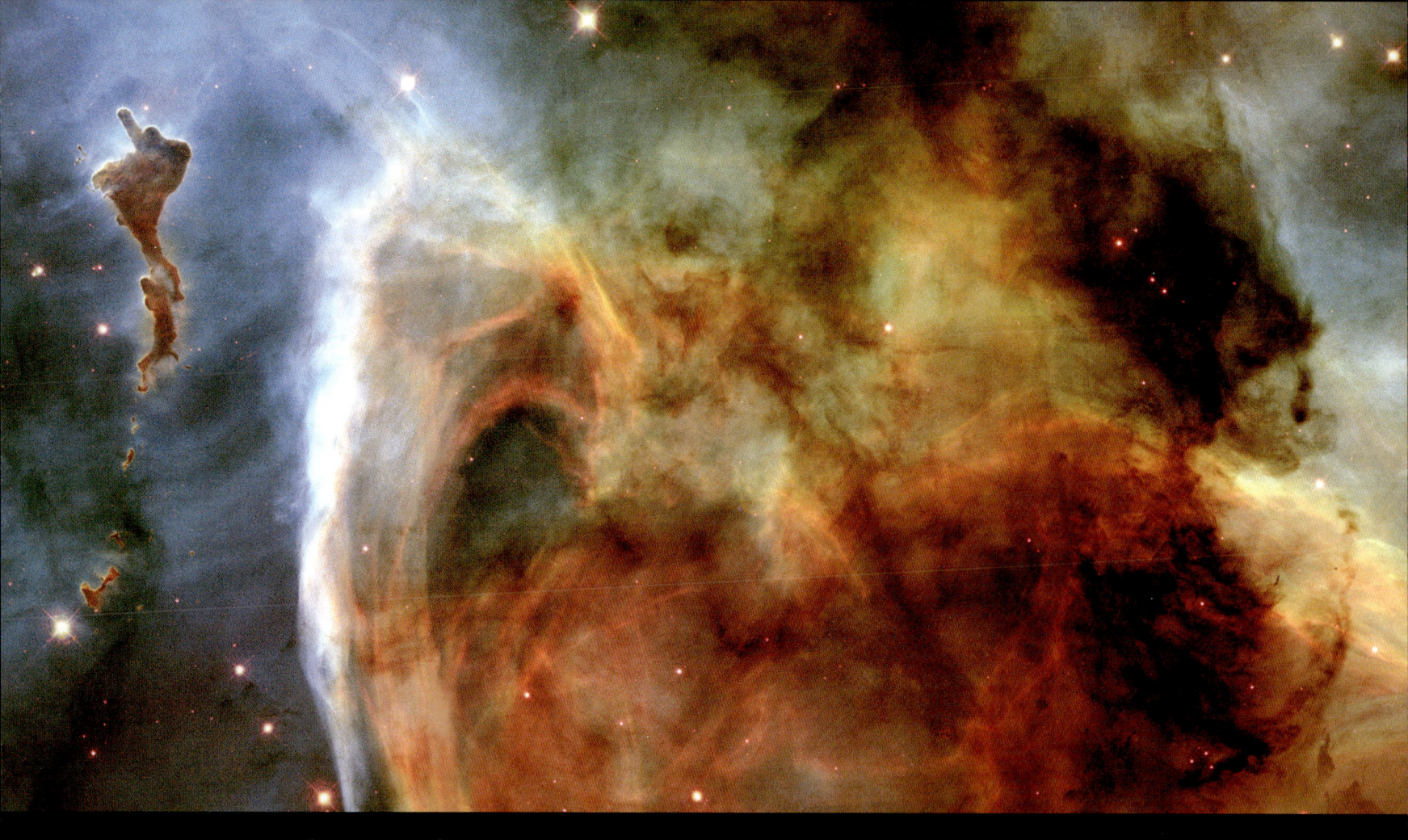

Keyhole Nebula

Previously unseen details of a mysterious, complex structure within the Carina Nebula are revealed by this image of the Keyhole Nebula. The circular keyhole structure contains bright filaments of hot, fluorescing gas as well as darkly silhouetted clouds of cold molecules and dust, all of which are in rapid, chaotic motion. Two strikingly large, sharp-edged dust clouds are located near the bottom center and upper left edges of the image. The former is immersed within the ring, and the latter is just outside the ring. The pronounced pillars and knobs of the upper left cloud appear to point toward a luminous, massive star located just outside the field farther toward the upper left, which may be responsible for illuminating and sculpting them by means of its high-energy radiation and stellar wind of high-velocity ejected material.

Mystic Mountain

This Hubble Space Telescope photograph captures the chaotic activity atop a three-light-year-tall pillar of gas and dust that is being eaten away by the brilliant light from nearby bright stars. This pillar within the Carina Nebula is also being assaulted from within, as stars buried inside it fire off jets of gas that can be seen streaming from towering peaks. Streamers of hot ionized gas can be seen flowing off the ridges of the structure, and wispy veils of dust, illuminated by starlight, float around its peaks.

NEBULAE: VEILS OF GLORY

By his spirit **he hath garnished the heavens.**

JOB 26:13

What melts our hearts is not just that there is beauty in the universe. **What melts us is the knowledge that God designed all beauty to show us who He is, as a symbolic language of the soul. All nature is God wooing us to Himself.**

STEPHEN MANSFIELD

Horsehead Nebula

The Horsehead Nebula is near Orion's belt. It's named after the distinct shape of opaque dust rising up in front of the emission nebula in the background. It glows red as a result of ultraviolet rays from stars that cause the gases to become electrically charged and glow. A broader view of the area, including Orion's belt, can be seen on page 135.

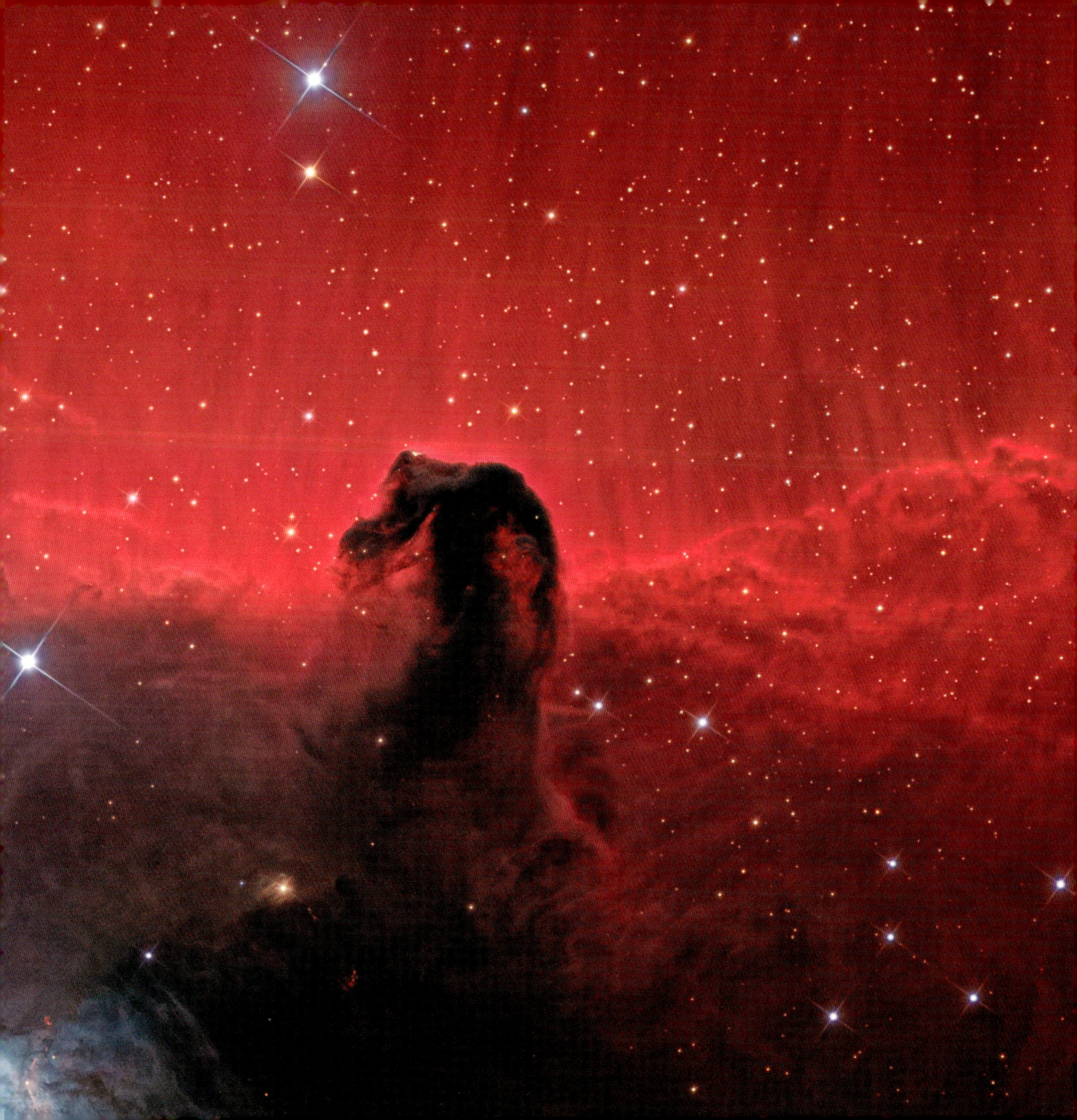

O LORD, thou hast searched me, and known me. Thou knowest my downsitting and mine uprising, thou understandest my thought afar off. Thou compassest my path and my lying down, and art acquainted with all my ways. For there is not a word in my tongue, but, lo, O LORD, thou knowest it altogether. Thou hast beset me behind and before, and laid thine hand upon me. *Such knowledge is too wonderful for me; it is high, I cannot attain unto it.*

PSALM 139:1–6

NGC 602

The high-energy radiation blazing out from the hot stars in this image of NGC 602 is sculpting the inner edge of the outer portions of the nebula, slowly eroding it away and eating into the material beyond. The diffuse outer reaches of the nebula prevent the energetic outflows from streaming away from the cluster. Ridges of dust and gaseous filaments are seen toward the northwest (in the upper-left part of the image) and toward the southeast (in the lower right-hand corner). Elephant trunk-like dust pillars point toward the hot blue stars and are telltale signs of the stars' eroding effect.

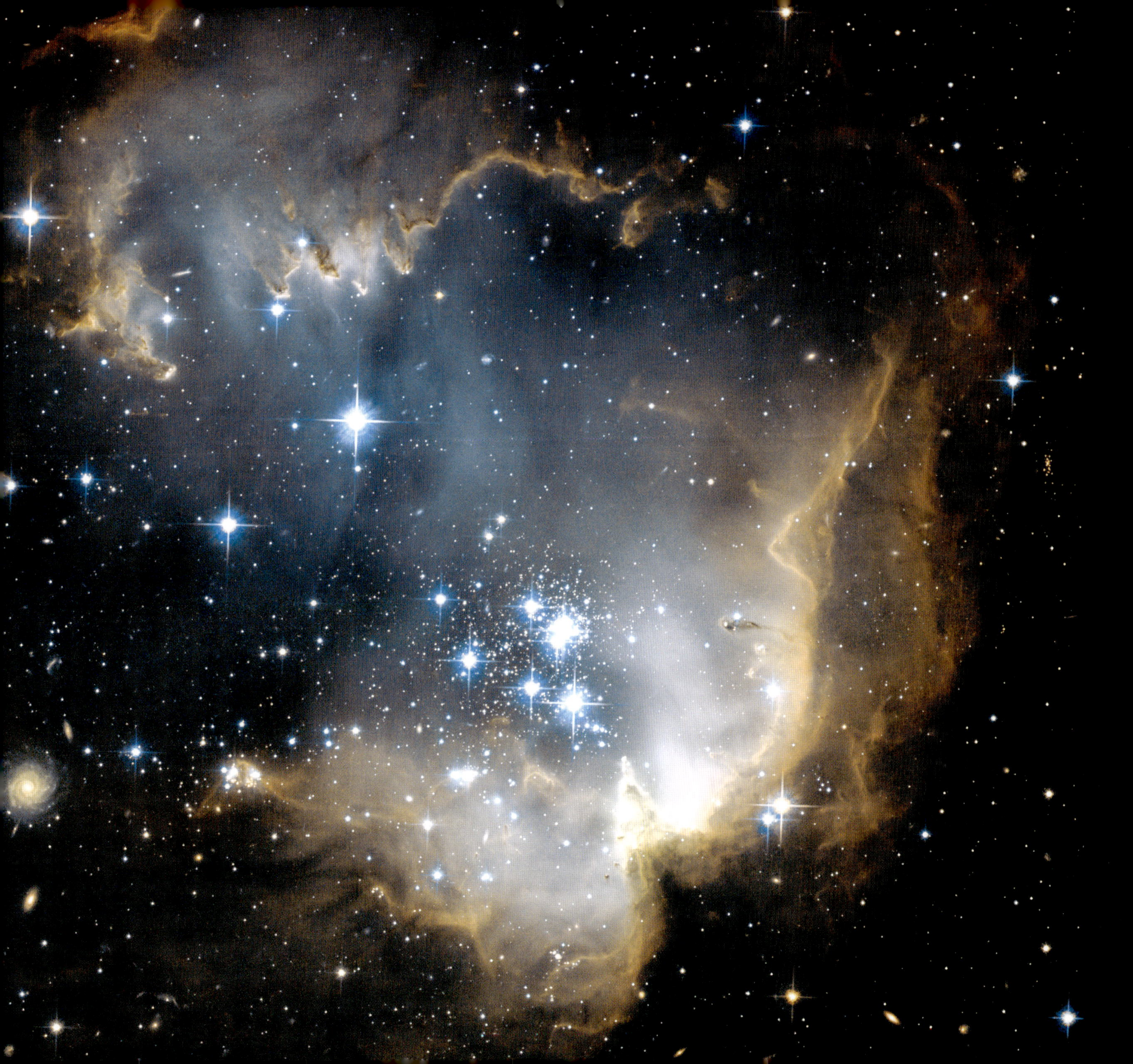

Omega Nebula

Resembling the fury of a raging sea, this image actually shows a bubbly ocean of glowing hydrogen gas and small amounts of other elements such as oxygen and sulfur. M17, also known as the Omega or Swan Nebula, is located about 5,500 light-years away in the constellation Sagittarius. The wave-like patterns of gas have been sculpted and illuminated by a torrent of ultraviolet radiation from young, massive stars, which lie outside the picture to the upper left. The glow of these patterns accentuates the three-dimensional structure of the gases. The ultraviolet radiation is carving and heating the surfaces of cold hydrogen gas clouds. The colors in the image represent various gases. Red represents sulfur; green, hydrogen; and blue, oxygen.

Small Magellanic Cloud

The Small Magellanic Cloud pictured here is a sparkling, star-packed dwarf galaxy that orbits the Milky Way. Although it is completely outside our galaxy and about 210,000 light-years away, it is still visible to the naked eye from the southern hemisphere.

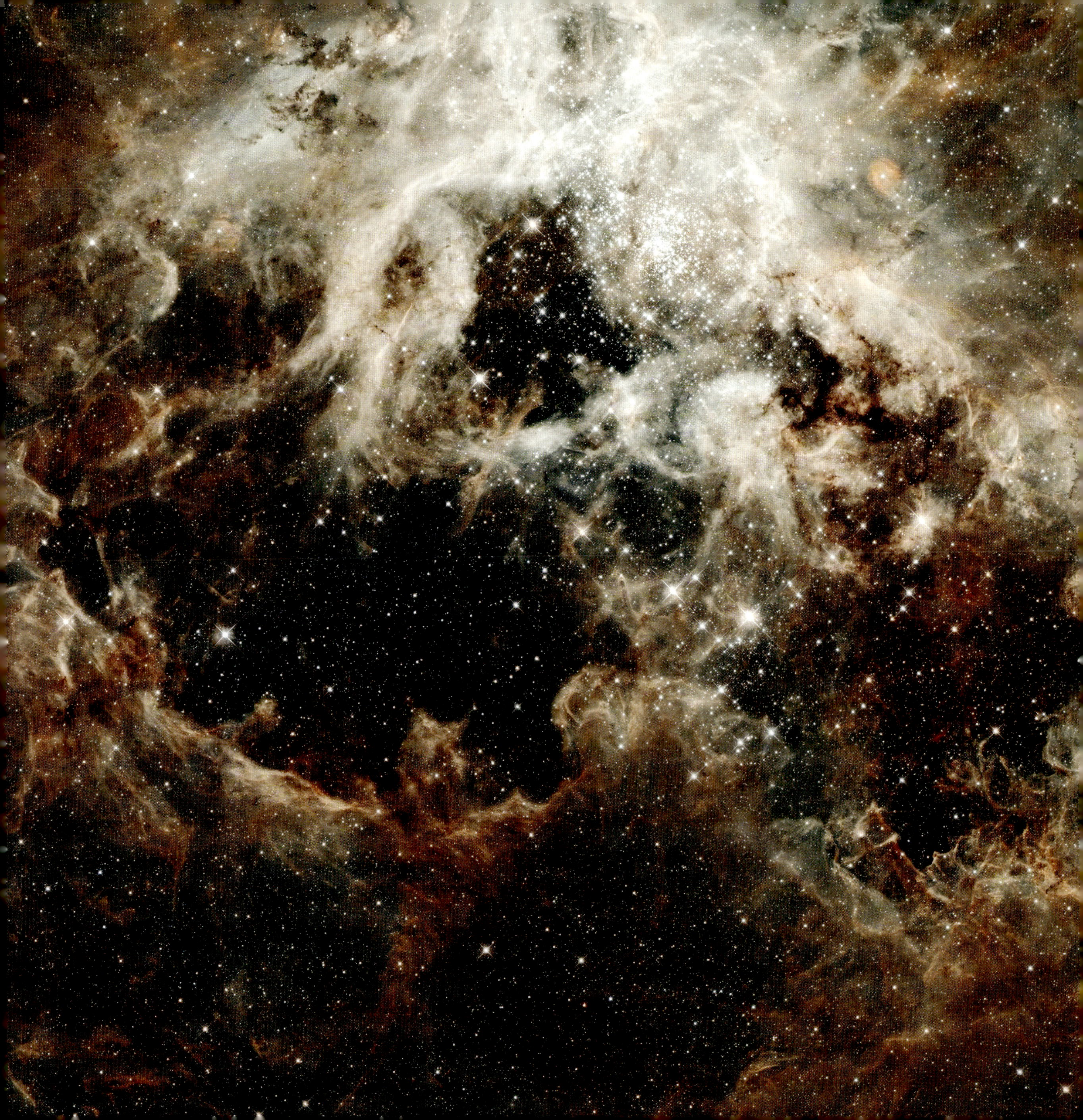

Tarantula Nebula

Several million young stars are vying for attention in this Hubble Space Telescope image of the Tarantula Nebula. The image reveals a fantasy landscape of pillars, ridges, and valleys. Early astronomers nicknamed this nebula the Tarantula because its glowing filaments resemble spider legs. The nebula resides 170,000 light-years away in the Large Magellanic Cloud, a small satellite galaxy of our Milky Way.

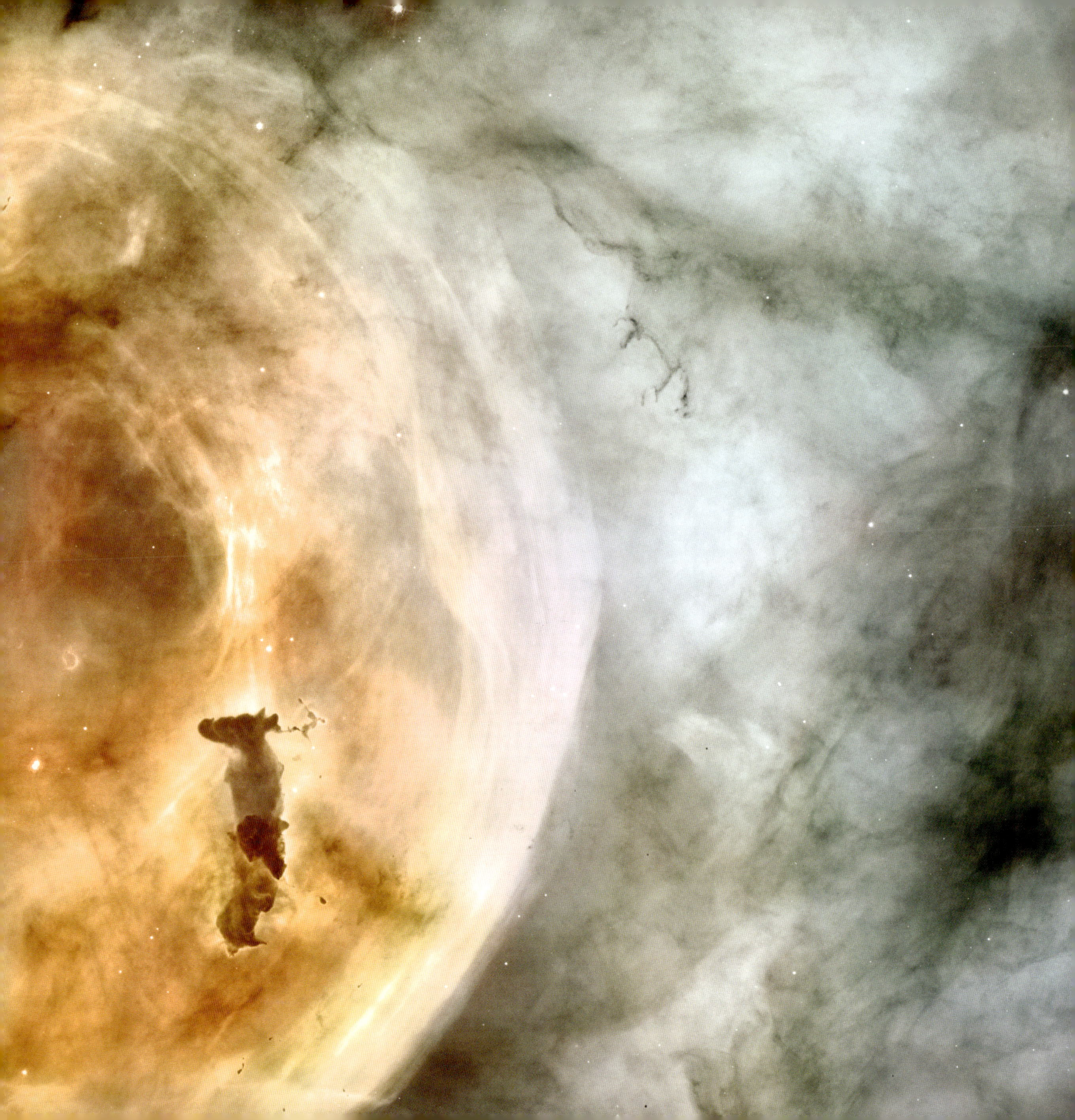

The Caterpillar and Celestial Marble

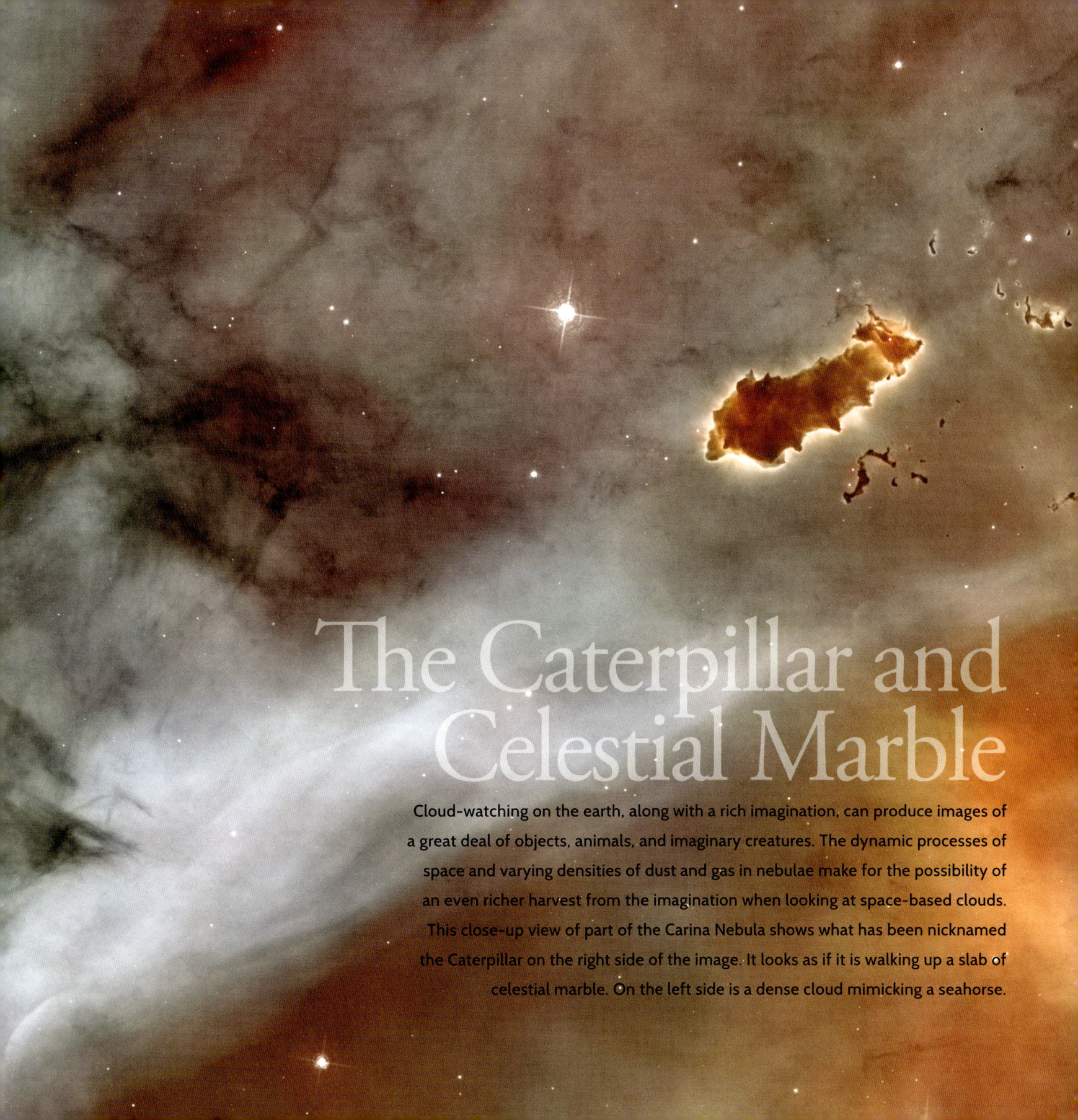

Cloud-watching on the earth, along with a rich imagination, can produce images of a great deal of objects, animals, and imaginary creatures. The dynamic processes of space and varying densities of dust and gas in nebulae make for the possibility of an even richer harvest from the imagination when looking at space-based clouds. This close-up view of part of the Carina Nebula shows what has been nicknamed the Caterpillar on the right side of the image. It looks as if it is walking up a slab of celestial marble. On the left side is a dense cloud mimicking a seahorse.

Trifid Nebula

This image shows the full Trifid Nebula. Dark lanes of dust are visible crisscrossing the center of it.

Located about 9,000 light-years from Earth, the Trifid Nebula resides in the constellation Sagittarius. A stellar jet (the thin, wispy object pointing to the upper left) protrudes from the head of a dense cloud and extends three-quarters of a light-year into the nebula. The jet's source is a very young stellar object that lies buried within the cloud.

For the eyes of the LORD run to and fro throughout the whole earth, **to shew himself strong** *in the behalf of them whose heart is perfect toward him.* 2 CHRONICLES 16:9A

Cometary Knots

Hubble was turned toward this area of sky to protect it from a hail of comet debris. These photos show how its view was filled with what appeared to be more comets but are actually streamers of dust and gas in the Helix Nebula. They are being pushed out by torrential radiation from the star that expelled them.

PLANETARY NEBULAE

Planetary nebulae form when a slowly dying star begins to throw off its outer layers, creating a beautiful halo of gas around it. Contrary to what the name suggests, this type of nebula is totally unrelated to the planets. Astronomers in the eighteenth century viewed these nebulae through their small telescopes. What they saw resembled planets; this is how the name originated. About 3,000 of these planetary nebulae are known to exist in our galaxy. The bright filaments of gas and the various colors of these nebulae usually can't be seen very well by directly observing through a telescope; they become evident only with long exposure astrophotography. Special filters that enhance wavelengths not detected in visible light are used at times too.

Both the Helix Nebula and the Hourglass Nebula are often referred to as "The Eye of God" because their unique structures give them the appearance of eyes. They can remind us that God sees everything that happens in His universe, and nothing that concerns us escapes His eye.

Planetary nebulae also demonstrate how God can create beauty from destruction. As these stars die, God creates far greater beauty from them. In the same way, we are transformed into glorious new creatures by the resurrection power of Christ when we die to ourselves and are quickened by His Spirit. This happens when we turn control of our lives over to Jesus. When we realize our smallness, that we are far too frail to control the world and what happens to us in it, then God gives us perfect peace and displays His beauty in our lives.

In November of 2002, the earth was on track to be bombarded with rocks from space which were left behind by a comet. Since Hubble was at risk and had to be protected during this meteor storm, astronomers turned the telescope to face away from the stream of debris for about a half day. And just as we have come to expect, regardless of whether we randomly look at a part of God's creation or intentionally pick a spot, we see glory and beauty. The Helix Nebula was almost directly opposite the incoming flow of meteors, so Hubble focused on the nebula and sent back some of the most incredible photographs of planetary nebulae ever taken. In hiding from the hail of comet debris, Hubble turned and filled its view with what appeared to be more comets. These enormous gaseous streamers have been dubbed "cometary knots" by astronomers, but they are much larger than any comet. The head of each one is at least twice the size of our entire solar system and the tails extend 100 billion miles, about 1,000 times the earth's distance from the sun.[1] They are being pushed away by blasts of hot gas and radiation surging from the star from which they themselves were ejected.[a]

---

[a] Some of the photographs were taken at times other than the 2002 meteor shower.

THE CELESTIAL MESSAGE

AGAIN

Helix Nebula

This photograph of the Helix Nebula is a combination of the photographs taken by Hubble and a photograph from a ground-based telescope. Planetary nebulae like the Helix are sculpted late in a star's life by a torrential gush of gases escaping from the dying star. Based on the nebula's distance of 650 light-years, its angular size corresponds to a huge ring with a diameter of nearly three light-years. That's approximately three-quarters of the distance between our sun and the next nearest star.

CAT'S EYE NEBULA Though the Cat's Eye Nebula was one of the first planetary nebulae to be discovered, it is still one of the most complex such nebulae ever seen in space. In 1994, Hubble first revealed the nebula's surprisingly intricate structures, including concentric gas shells, jets of high-speed gas, and unusual shock-induced knots of gas. Each 'ring' is actually the edge of a spherical bubble seen projected onto the sky—that's why it appears bright along its outer edge.

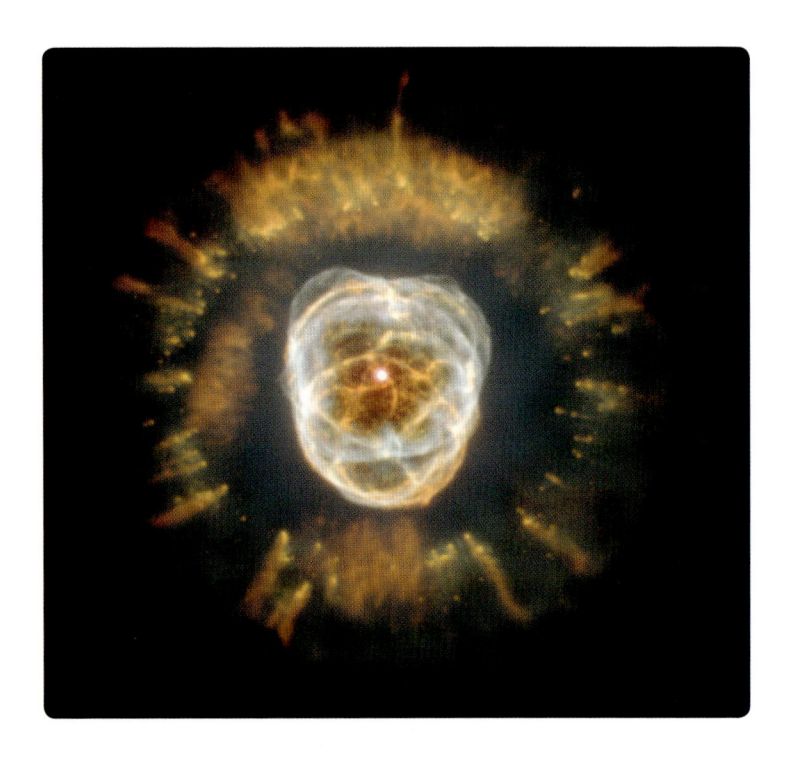

ESKIMO NEBULA This stellar relic is nicknamed the Eskimo Nebula because when viewed through ground-based telescopes, it resembles a face surrounded by a fur parka. This Hubble telescope image shows that the "parka" is really a disk of material embellished with a ring of comet-shaped objects, their tails streaming away from the central, dying star. The Eskimo's "face" also contains some fascinating details. Although this bright central region resembles a ball of twine, it is actually a bubble of material being blown into space by the central star's intense "wind" of high-speed material.

THE CELESTIAL MESSAGE

Bubble Nebula

It's strange enough to find a star that can blow bubbles, but even more unbelievable that the bubble is about 10 light-years wide! That's big enough to stretch more than 10,000 solar systems across. Not only is the bubble big, but the star that made it is exceptionally powerful as well. At 40 times more massive than the sun and hundreds of thousands of times more luminous, the Bubble Nebula is a fit candidate for blowing colossal bubbles.

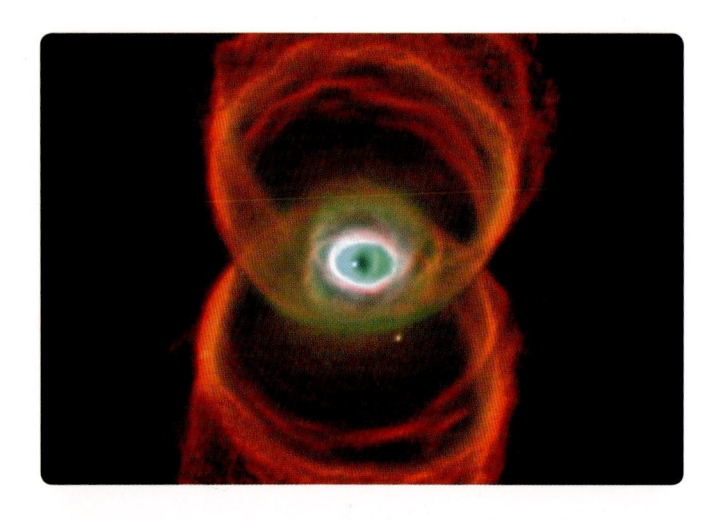

HOURGLASS NEBULA Astronomers looking at this nebula were met with a returning gaze from the "eye" at its center. This eye is always turned our direction, reminding us of the all-seeing eye of God that runs to and fro across the earth. This is called the Hourglass Nebula because of its overall shape.

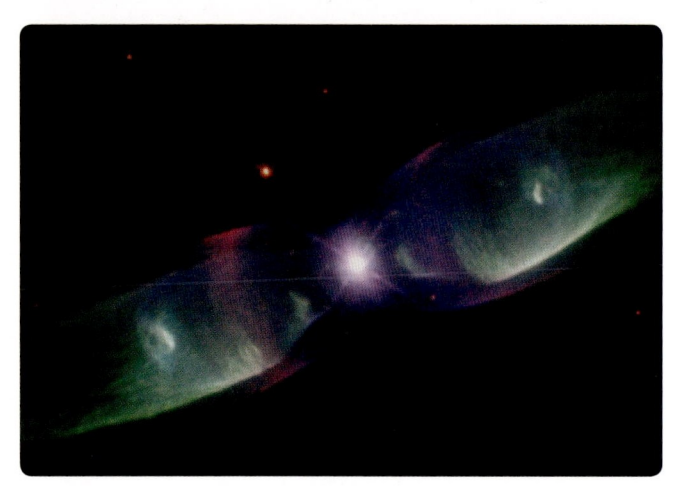

M2-9 is a striking example of a "butterfly" or a bipolar planetary nebula. Another more revealing name might be the Twin Jet Nebula. If the nebula would be sliced across the star, the two sides would appear much like a pair of exhausts from jet engines. Indeed, because of the nebula's shape and the measured velocity of the gas, in excess of 200 miles per second, astronomers believe that the description as a super-supersonic jet exhaust is quite apt.

HD 44179 This nebula is called the Red Rectangle because of its appearance in ground-based telescopes. The Hubble Space Telescope took this image that shows more detail and reveals that the symmetrical shape is most likely caused by two jets of gas being expelled from the central star. The expanding rings of gas are oriented with the edges facing us so we see them as straight lines rather than circles.

Butterfly Nebula

This nebula looks like a delicate butterfly. But it is far from serene. What resembles dainty butterfly wings are actually roiling cauldrons of gas heated to more than 36,000 degrees Fahrenheit. The gas is tearing across space at more than 600,000 miles an hour—fast enough to travel from Earth to the moon in 24 minutes! A dying star that was once about five times the mass of the sun is at the center of this fury. It has ejected its envelope of gases and is now unleashing a stream of ultraviolet radiation that makes the cast-off material glow.

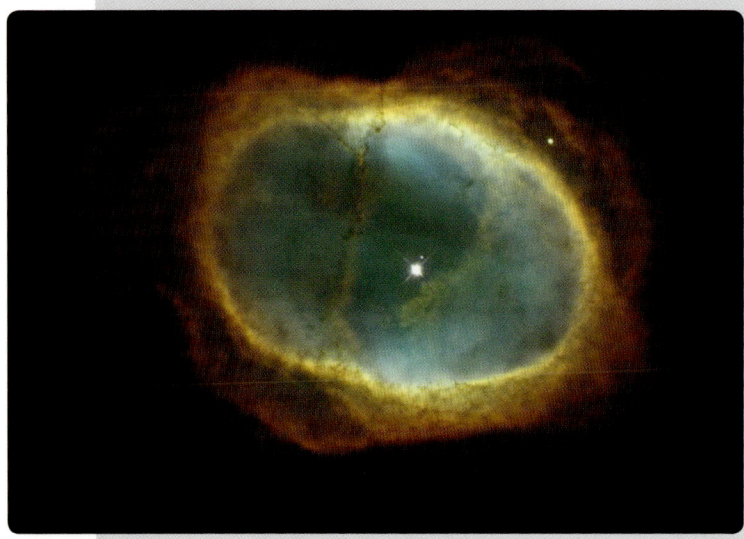

Top: A close up view of the center of NGC 2440 shows a soft halo of beauty around the remains of a star.

Middle: This striking image of NGC 3132, also known as the Southern Ring Nebula, shows another gem of splendor in the universe God has created. This giant jewel is nearly three trillion miles across and is expanding outward from the central star at nine miles per second. Although we are witnessing the destruction of a star, Almighty God transforms this devastation into splendor in the same way that He extracts beauty from ashes.

Bottom: This image of NGC 2440, taken by NASA's Hubble Space Telescope, shows the colorful "last hurrah" of a star like our sun. The star's life is ending as it casts off its outer layers of gas, which formed a cocoon around the star's remaining core. Ultraviolet light from the dying star makes the material glow. The burned-out star, called a white dwarf, is the white dot in the center.

Right: Planetary nebulae, such as NGC 5189 here, represent the final brief stage in the life of a medium-sized star like our sun. While consuming the last of the fuel in its core, the dying star expels a large portion of its outer envelope. This material then becomes heated by the radiation from the stellar remnant and radiates, displaying glowing clouds of gas in complex patterns, since the ejection of mass from the star is uneven in both time and direction.

NGC 5189

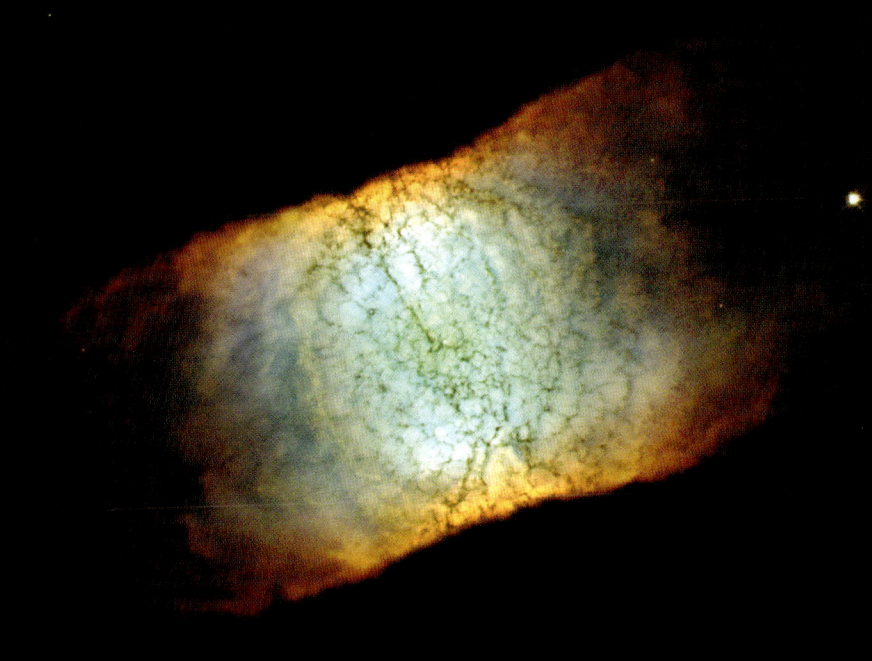

Retina Nebula

If we could fly around the Retina Nebula in a starship, we would see that the gas and dust form a vast doughnut of material streaming outward from the dying star. From Earth, we view the doughnut from the side. This side view allows us to see the intricate tendrils of dust that have been compared to the eye's retina. The dust lanes are like a rather open mesh veil wrapped around the bright doughnut. In other planetary nebulae, like the Ring Nebula on the next page, we view the doughnut from the top.

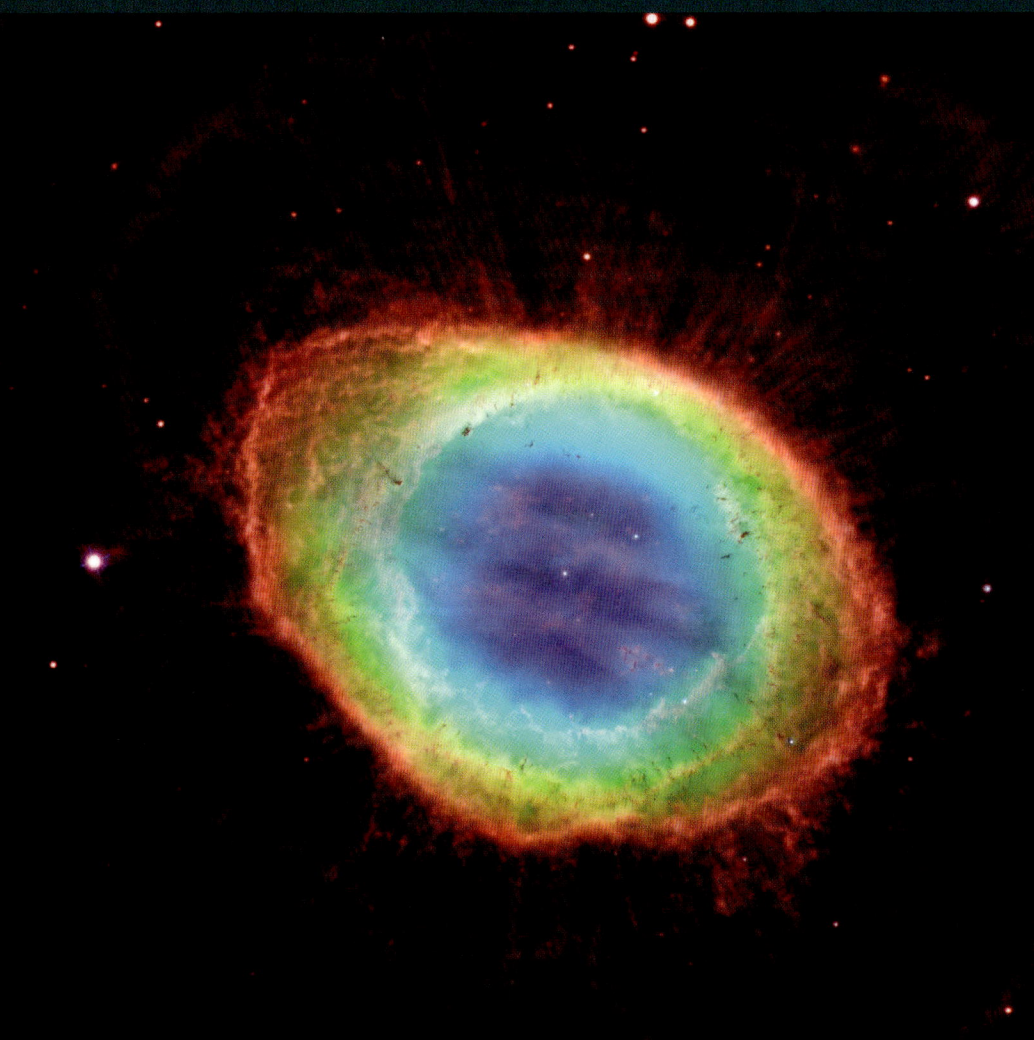

Ring Nebula

The Ring Nebula, the most famous of all planetary nebulae, is displayed here in the sharpest photograph ever taken of it. This nebula is almost identical to the Retina Nebula on the previous page except that it is being viewed from the top and through the hole of the doughnut. This photograph gives a nearly three-dimensional view of the dust veil mesh that's wrapped around the doughnut.

NEBULAE: VEILS OF GLORY

S106

The view presented here has been compared to a "soaring, celestial snow angel." This nebula, S106, has two lobes of super-hot gas billowing out from the parent star that form the two wings of the angel. Red dust stretches underneath, between, and above the wings to finish out the impression, giving us an out-of-this-world angel.

Honour and majesty are before him: **strength and beauty are in his sanctuary.** PSALM 96:6

128   THE CELESTIAL MESSAGE

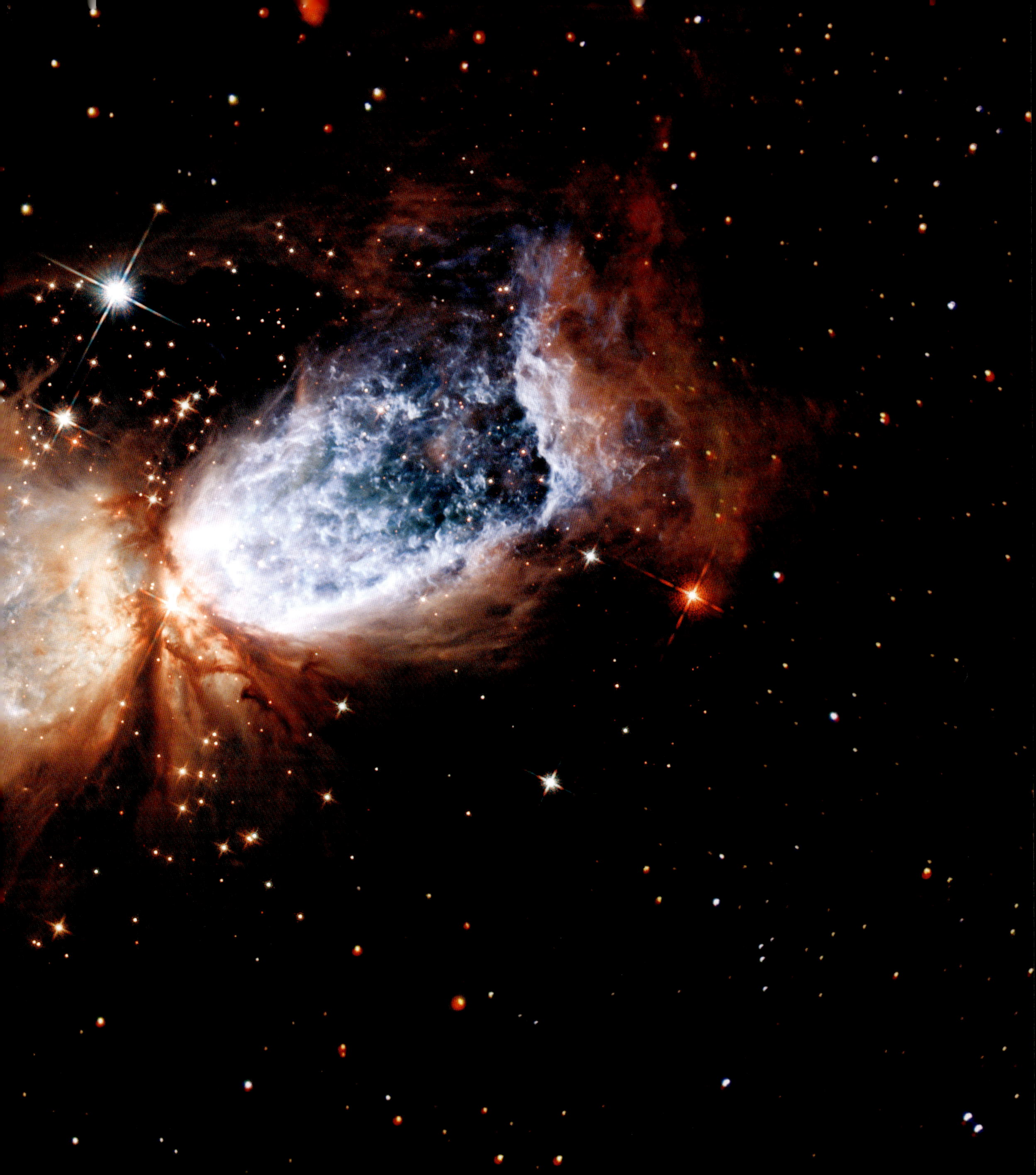

V838 Monocerotis

In January 2002, V838 Monocerotis, a dull star in an obscure constellation, suddenly became 600,000 times more luminous than our sun, temporarily making it the brightest star in our Milky Way Galaxy. The mysterious star has long since faded back to obscurity, but observations by NASA's Hubble Space Telescope of a phenomenon called a "light echo" have uncovered remarkable new features. These details promise to provide astronomers with a CAT-scan-like probe of the three-dimensional structure of shells of dust surrounding an aging star.

May 20, 2002

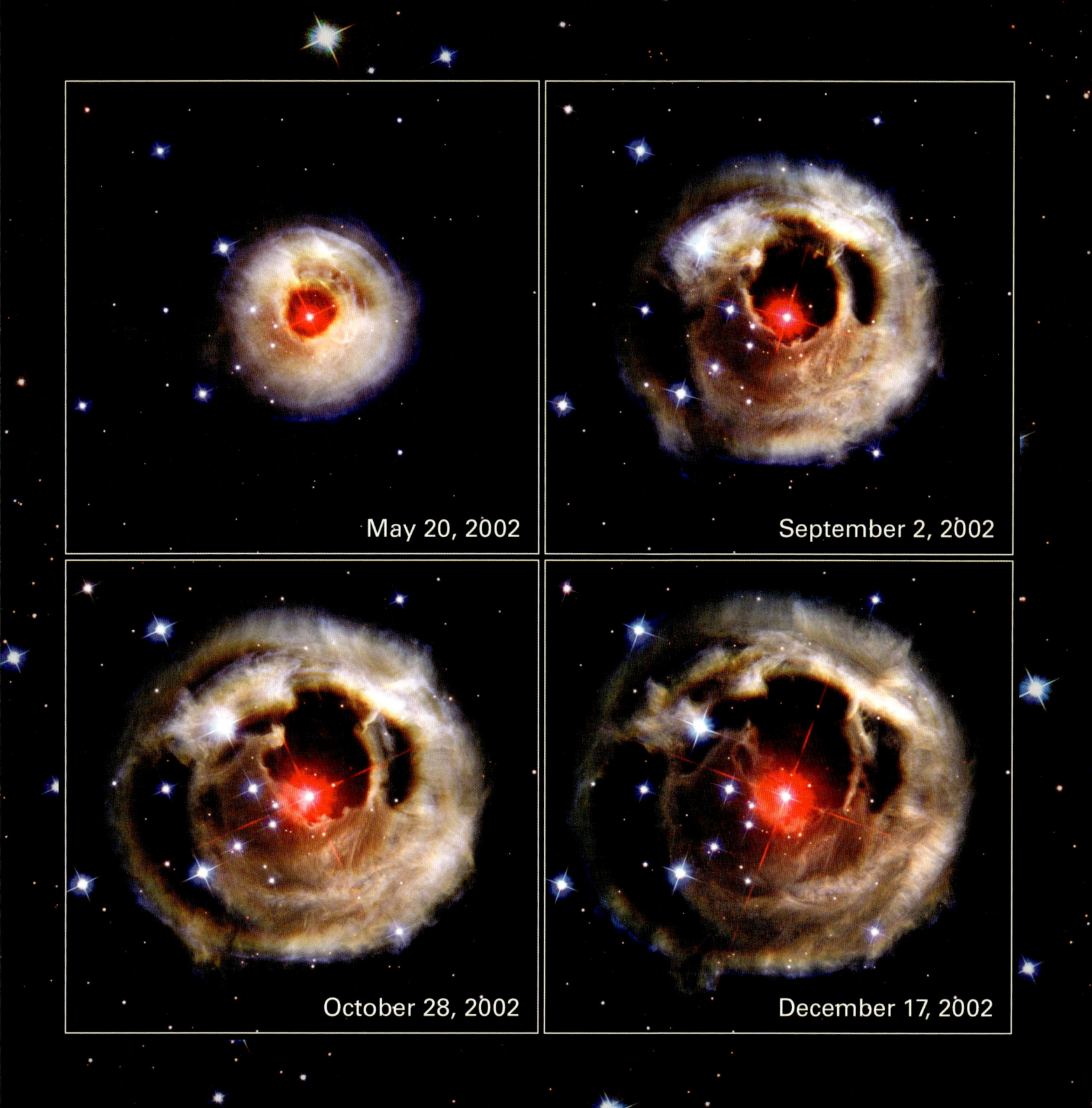

September 2, 2002

October 28, 2002

December 17, 2002

The Hubble Space Telescope floats gracefully above the blue Earth after release from the space shuttle Discovery's robotic arm at the conclusion of a successful servicing mission. As the cosmos is magnified by this instrument of science, the Lord is magnified through the discovery of His marvelous works.

chapter six
The View

Let's imagine that we have an open evening and we've decided to spend it outside stargazing. First we grab the telescope, right? Then we add our battery pack, case of lenses, the star maps, dew shield, mosquito spray, and flashlight. Won't all these things add to the experience?

These are all tools to help us observe, but they are not the most important ones. We don't need fancy, high-tech equipment to have an enjoyable evening under the stars. All we need are our eyes. There are lots of things we can see without a telescope. Things such as constellations and meteor showers are best seen with no telescope at all. If you are in a dark sky location, you can even see a faint galaxy or two.

The eye is an amazing tool God has given us so that we can enjoy the wonders of His creation. The eye is even made in a way that it can optimize itself for seeing in the dark.

The first thing that happens after we step out into the darkness of night is that our pupils dilate, or open widely. This process is finished after only a couple of seconds. Next, chemical changes start to take place in the eye. The cone cells in the eye start adapting to the low light levels, taking close to 10 minutes to make the full transition. When that happens, our eyes are almost completely adapted to the dark. But the eye still has one more trick to make it even a bit more sensitive. The rod cells in the eye begin to dark-adapt, reaching full sensitivity after about 30 minutes. When all these changes have taken place, our eyes are over 10,000 times more sensitive than they are in full daylight. So, to get the full benefit of viewing the stars, be sure your eyes have plenty of time to adapt to the darkness, and you will be able to see many more stars than you will if you just step outside briefly.

The Creator will always receive glory for everything He sets out to do and for everything He makes. Our eyes are no exception. He receives glory directly for the exquisite design of the eye and indirectly by all the scenes our eyes can view. When we use these incredible tools to scan the heavens, God is glorified once again. When we recognize the tremendous power and massive size of the stars, and then, in turn, give recognition to God for what we see, we bring Him honor. More simply stated, when we see what He has made and praise Him for it, the purpose of its creation is being fulfilled.

The stars can fill us with overwhelming awe. In Psalm 19, David tells how the stars declare God's glory. Mankind, in any part of the earth, can look up and understand this language. "The heavens declare the glory of God; and the firmament sheweth his handiwork. Day unto day uttereth speech, and night unto night sheweth knowledge. There is no speech nor language, where their voice is not heard. Their line is gone out through all the earth, and their words to the end of the world" (Psalm 19:1–4a).

Some of the star groupings that we can see without the help

> *Seek him that maketh the seven stars and Orion ...* **The LORD is his name.**
>
> AMOS 5:8

of optics are mentioned in the Bible. Job 38:31 says, "Canst thou bind the sweet influences of Pleiades, or loose the bands of Orion?" Pleiades is a beautiful open cluster of stars also known as the Seven Sisters. God appears to be asking Job if he could bind the cluster and stop its expansion. Orion is a constellation that can be seen in the evening in winter. It has a distinctive line of three bright stars across its midsection. God was asking Job if he could "loose the bands," or take off Orion's belt.

Meteor showers are also best when viewed without optical aids. A telescope is basically useless in a meteor shower since meteors can appear from any direction in the sky, at any given time, and last only a few seconds at most.

The God who decided to create an amazing universe has enabled us to enjoy it by blessing us with an equally amazing set of eyes. Let's use them!

As stars shine, their beams of light fan out across space and travel billions of miles undisturbed. The rays can travel for hundreds and even thousands of years in pristine condition until the final second when they strike the earth's atmosphere. Then they instantly become muddled and distorted. Fine detail is lost as the light passes through this haze of air molecules, vapor, and dust. This is why the stars appear to twinkle. It gives them an enchanting appearance, but it causes the view from an earth-based telescope to be spoiled. Astronomers wanted to have a view from above the atmosphere to avoid this problem.

The Hubble Space Telescope was the answer. As it orbits 350 miles above Earth, it is far above the distorting effects of the atmosphere below. However, when the telescope was first launched in 1990, there was an obvious problem. The images coming back from it were not nearly as sharp as astronomers had hoped for. After extensive testing, it was discovered that Hubble's large 94-inch primary mirror was flawed. It had been ground too flat by a mere one-fiftieth of the width of a human hair.[1] Unlike earth-bound telescopes, Hubble's vision was limited only by its optics, so the optical aberration was very noticeable. The telescope was almost a complete failure, but a remedy was being planned. A corrective optics package was designed and later installed on the first servicing mission to the telescope. The results were phenomenal; Hubble was wearing prescription lenses and could now see clearly! According to NASA, Hubble's keen vision is equivalent to standing at the U.S. Capitol and seeing the date on a quarter at the Washington Monument a mile away. This instrument opened our eyes to the spectacular wonders of the universe around us as it sent back thousands of beautiful images that dazzle the senses. And every image it sends reaffirms that "the heavens declare the glory of God."

Belt of Orion

Alnitak, Alnilam, and Mintaka are the bright bluish stars from left to right in this gorgeous cosmic vista. Otherwise known as the Belt of Orion, these three blue supergiant stars are hotter and much more massive than the sun. Clouds of gas and dust adrift in this region have intriguing and some surprisingly familiar shapes, including the dark Horsehead Nebula and Flame Nebula near Alnitak at the lower left.

If the stars should appear but one night every thousand years, how man would marvel and stare.
RALPH WALDO EMERSON

Instead, they come out every night, and we read the newspaper.

Top: This comparison image of the core of galaxy M100 shows the dramatic improvement in the Hubble telescope's view of the universe. The new image (right) was taken with the second generation Wide Field and Planetary Camera, which was installed during the STS-61 Hubble Servicing Mission.

Left: The brilliant stars seen in this image are members of the popular open star cluster known as Pleiades, or the Seven Sisters.

Zeta Ophiuchi

The blue star near the center of this image, Zeta Ophiuchi, is a runaway star plowing through space dust. When seen in visible light, it appears as a relatively dim red star surrounded by other dim stars and no dust. However, in this infrared image, a completely different view emerges. Zeta Ophiuchi is actually a very massive, bright blue star plowing its way through a large cloud of interstellar dust and gas.

chapter seven
Light and Creation

On day one of Creation, God called for light to appear, and it has been with us since. Light seems so simple, yet it is extremely complex and interesting. Light is made of particles like miniature bullets but behaves like waves. Light carries every one of the colors of the spectrum, but when these colors are combined in full spectrum light, we see no color at all.

We cannot see many of light's properties. On one side of the visible spectrum, just beyond the deepest color of red, our eyes lose sensitivity. Here lies the **infrared** part of the spectrum. This part of light can carry heat. A little farther over are microwaves, the type of radiation used in microwave ovens. Microwaves excite certain molecules, such as those in water and food, causing them to spin, creating heat. Farther yet on this side of the spectrum are radio waves, which carry cellular phone signals. How many people realize that light is carrying their voices during a phone conversation? If we return to the other side of the visible spectrum, just beyond the deepest shade of purple, we get to ultraviolet rays. These can burn your skin after prolonged exposure. Next to those are X-rays. These freely pass through our bodies, allowing doctors to image broken bones that can't be seen. Each of these wavelengths of light offers unique information. Astronomers use them to gather more information by using telescopes that hone in on the invisible parts of the light spectrum.

All objects that we can see are revealed to us by photons bouncing off the objects and landing in our eyes. So in reality, when we look at things around us, we are not directly seeing the objects, but only the impression or imprint left by the photons on our retinas. For example, we can walk into a dark room that has a single chair and see nothing. But the instant we turn on the light in the room, we can detect the chair. Turn off the light, and it disappears. The only thing that has changed is the absence of light. This illustrates that we are not seeing the chair directly, but only photons that have left the light bulb, bounced off the chair, and landed in our eyes. The image we see is not five feet away where the chair sits; rather, it's in the eye of the beholder. We may think we're the ones seeing into the distance, but in reality, light brings the distance to us! It may seem mind-boggling to think that everything we see is literally in our eyes, but the brain adds a sense of dimensions and depth perception to make objects appear to be outside our eyes and off in the distance as they are in reality.

Yet, technically, we aren't seeing objects but only light itself. This helps us understand how our view of the sun, moon and stars reveals them as they were in the past.

DISTANT STARLIGHT

Light travels at approximately 186,000 miles per second. Since the moon is about 238,857 miles from the earth, it takes light 1.3 seconds to travel this distance. The sun is approximately 93

| Penetrates Earth's Atmosphere? | Y | N | Y | N |

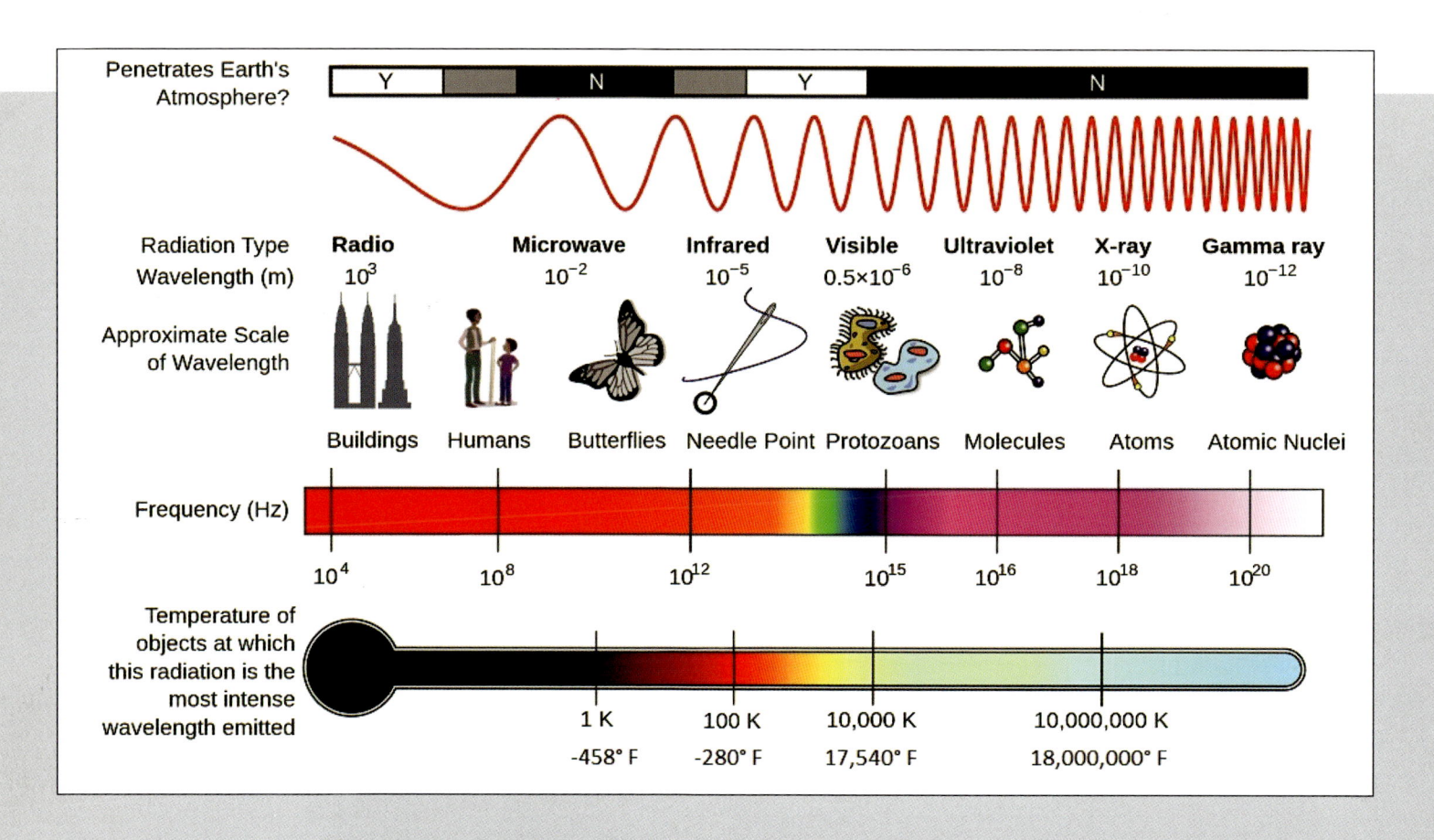

Radiation Type	Radio	Microwave	Infrared	Visible	Ultraviolet	X-ray	Gamma ray
Wavelength (m)	10^3	10^{-2}	10^{-5}	0.5×10^{-6}	10^{-8}	10^{-10}	10^{-12}
Approximate Scale of Wavelength	Buildings	Humans / Butterflies	Needle Point	Protozoans	Molecules	Atoms	Atomic Nuclei

Frequency (Hz): 10^4, 10^8, 10^{12}, 10^{15}, 10^{16}, 10^{18}, 10^{20}

Temperature of objects at which this radiation is the most intense wavelength emitted:
1 K / −458° F
100 K / −280° F
10,000 K / 17,540° F
10,000,000 K / 18,000,000° F

Top: The **electromagnetic spectrum** is the range of all frequencies of radiation; this includes visible light and all other types of radiation from radio waves to gamma rays. Human eyes are sensitive only to the multicolored region of visible light in the center. However, astronomers can build a wide variety of telescopes that are able to detect all of the wavelengths in this spectrum. This gives valuable information that is not evident when viewing astronomical objects in visible light alone.

Opposite page: Why does this galaxy emit such spectacular jets? No one is sure, but it is likely related to an active supermassive black hole at its center. The galaxy at the image center, Hercules A, appears to be a relatively normal elliptical galaxy in visible light. When imaged in radio waves, however, tremendous plasma jets over one million light-years long appear. Detailed analyses indicate that the central galaxy is actually over 1,000 times more massive than our Milky Way Galaxy, and the central black hole is nearly 1,000 times more massive than the black hole at the Milky Way's center. The physics that create the jets remain a topic of research. The likely source of energy is inward-falling matter swirling toward the central black hole.

THE CELESTIAL MESSAGE

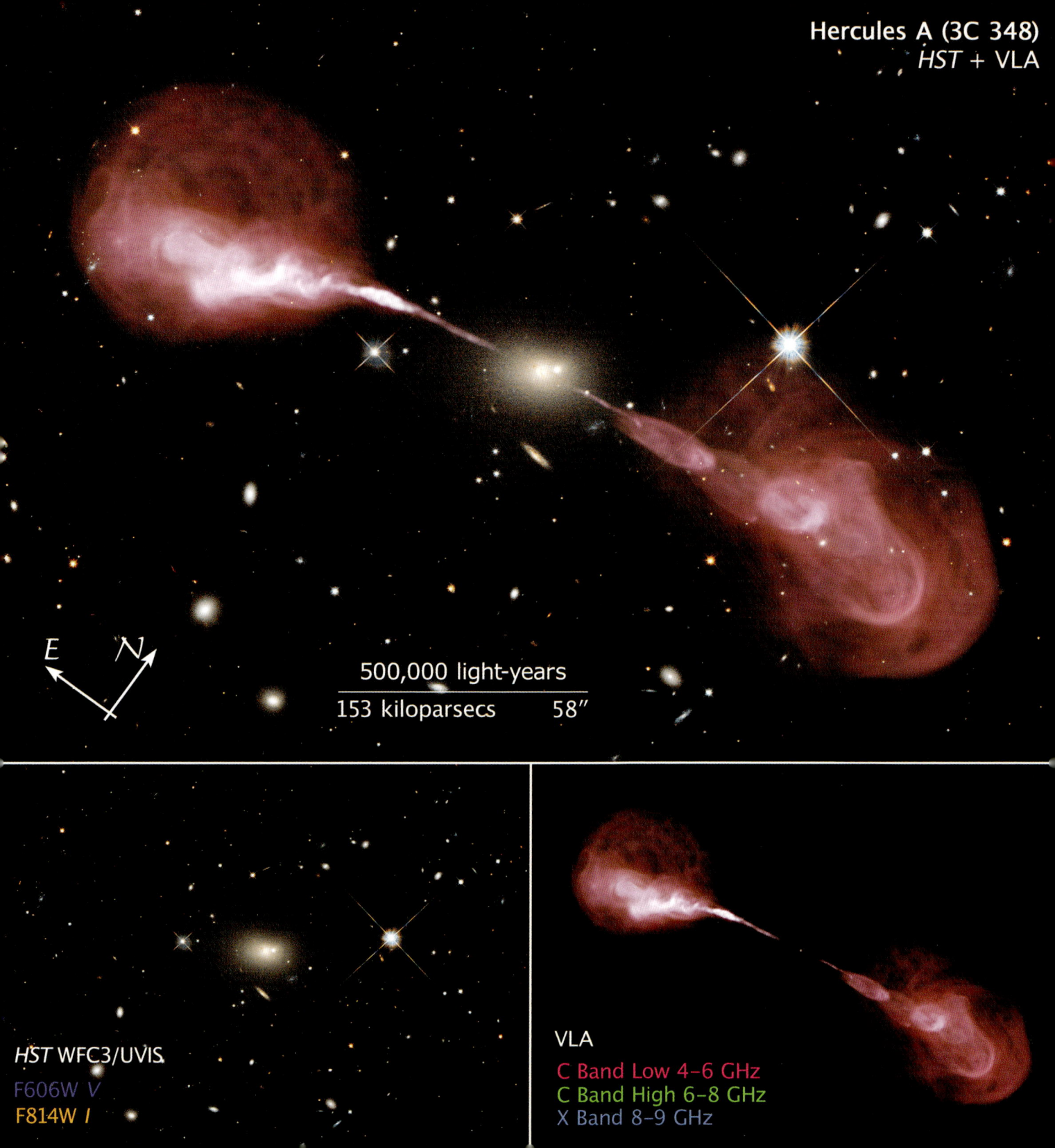

Hercules A (3C 348)
HST + VLA

500,000 light-years
153 kiloparsecs
58"

HST WFC3/UVIS
F606W V
F814W I

VLA
C Band Low 4–6 GHz
C Band High 6–8 GHz
X Band 8–9 GHz

This photo shows the strong outpouring of light and gases flowing from VY Canis Majoris, one of the largest known stars in the universe.

In many ways, light is symbolic of God. Both present us with mysteries. Just as we do not completely understand how we can see the light of distant stars, neither can we fully comprehend the One who created that light.

million miles from the earth, and light traveling this distance takes about eight minutes. Because of this, we never see the sun as it is currently, but rather how it was eight minutes in the past. The stars are much farther away, so the travel time is proportionately longer. Proxima Centauri lies at a distance that takes light 4.2 years to cover. This means that it is possible to "travel" into the past to view history if we only look far enough off into the distance. Who knew that stargazers were also time travelers?

As always, when we learn more about God's wonderful creation, we face mysteries that are hard to explain. They remind us that the more we know, the more we realize we don't know. These mysteries are not a surprise, as the entire Creation process was a miracle far beyond our ability to fathom.

One of the mysteries we face is how light could have traveled across millions of light-years of space and still have reached the earth in the short time since Creation. Many stars are too far away for the light from them, traveling at normal speeds, to have reached us in the approximately 6,000 years since Creation.

We must remember that God made a fully mature creation. Consequently there was a practical appearance of age everywhere, in man, animals, the Garden of Eden, and the stars. So we should expect to see this appearance of age when we look back in time through telescopes, even if we could look all the way back to Creation.

God didn't place Adam in a barren Garden of Eden with seeds just beginning to sprout. When Adam woke up and took the first breath of life, he viewed mature grasses, fruit trees, and other vegetation. As he began to understand the principles of plant growth, Adam could have looked at a towering tree that appeared to be 100 years old and thought, *It is impossible that God created this tree just a few days ago; the evidence points to this tree being very old!*

Some people today reach this type of conclusion as they look millions of light-years into the universe. But there was a reason why the infant tree next to Adam had the appearance of age; God made it that way because He wanted a mature and beautiful creation that was already finished on day six, and He didn't want Adam—the pinnacle of His creation—to wake up in a barren desert with life just starting to break through the surface. In the same way, there is a reason we can see the light from distant stars. God made the heavenly bodies for measuring time on Earth and to bring glory to Himself, so of course He would see to it that they would be visible from the very beginning.

> *The heavens declare his righteousness,*
> **and all the people see his glory.**
>
> PSALM 97:6

Some astronomers have suggested that God could also have brought light to the earth through purely natural processes, without bending the laws of physics, or in other words, invoking a miracle. Creationists such as Dr. Russell Humphreys and Dr. John Hartnett have postulated several natural processes God could have used to get distant starlight to Earth. These involve gravitational time dilation, which means that the flow of time itself is altered in certain areas of the universe as a result of the distribution of mass. Gravitational time dilation was first postulated by Einstein in his Special Theory of Relativity. It is something that has been experimentally observed to be happening around us in a small way even today. The key ingredient that makes gravitational time dilation bring starlight to the earth quickly is the expansion of the universe. This expansion is not just an assumption; it's something that we clearly see happening in the cosmos. Something is causing the universe to spread out. Interestingly enough, the Bible tells us that God is doing exactly that! See footnote on page 12.

CREATION

The **Big Bang Theory** was first proposed in the early 1900s as an explanation for the origin of the universe. It stated that all the matter and energy in the universe originated from a state of enormous density and temperature that exploded at a finite moment in the past. When the Big Bang Theory was proposed, almost all major **cosmologists** accepted the Steady State Theory, which stated that the universe had no beginning. However, astronomers began to reject this theory as they began to see overwhelming evidence of a beginning to the universe. The Big Bang Theory then became more and more accepted as an explanation of how the universe could have started. It was actually a step in the right direction because it acknowledges one thing the Bible says—the universe had a beginning. Yet the Big Bang Theory denies the role of an intelligent Creator and falls far short of answering the many questions of how a universe could make itself.

The **Cosmic Microwave Background** (CMB) presents the Big Bang Theory with a problem. The CMB is the background radiation that has been detected in every direction around us. It shows the radiation distributed very evenly, much more so than it should be even in the 14-billion-year time frame of the Big Bang. So the question remains. How did light and heat move across the universe to create the even temperatures seen in the CMB? Even the Big Bang with its billions of years does not allow for enough time to correspond with the even distribution of light and heat we see today. This is termed the "horizon problem."

The attempted solution to this difficulty was the "**inflation model.**" This states that the universe expanded at a "normal" rate after the Big Bang occurred, allowing points of the universe to exchange energy. After this, it abruptly underwent a rapid inflation phase where the areas of the universe were pushed far apart. The inflation was then somehow turned off and the expansion

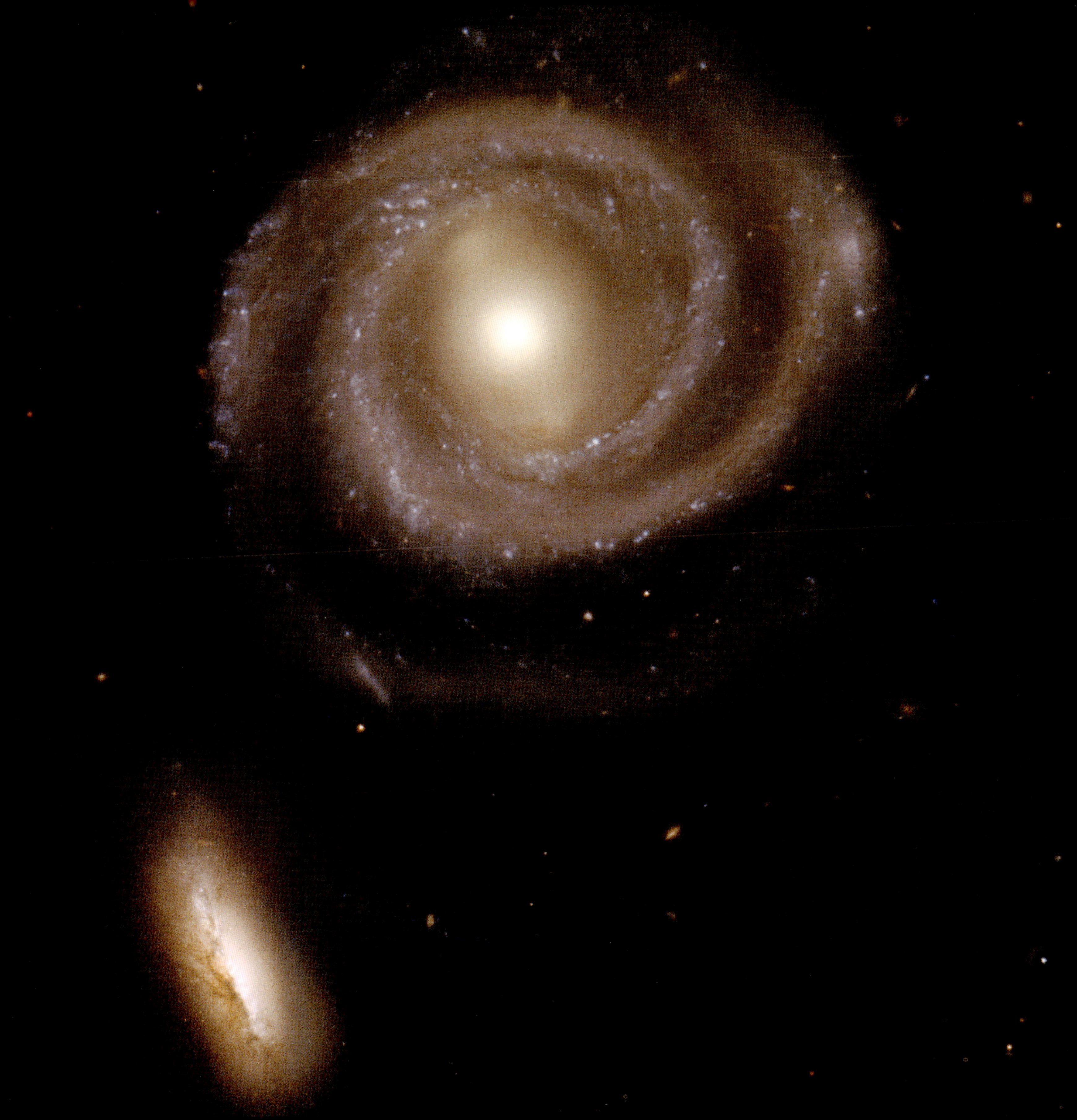

NGC 5754

This photo shows the large galaxy NGC 5754 and the smaller NGC 5752 as they interact with each other through their gravitational attraction. The currently winding spiral arms of galaxies like NGC 5754 testify to a relatively recent creation as they would be wound up beyond recognition if they were billions of years old.

reverted to the normal rate.[1]

The many suppositions in the Big Bang Theory show us that even man's best explanations leave many unsolved and unanswered questions. Since God's ways are above man's ways, we will never be able to fully comprehend the workings of the universe. God is omnipotent. He is not limited! Therefore, our human reasoning should not limit Him to our comprehension of things. If our weak minds are perplexed by things we do not understand, this does not change the facts about God. He remains all-powerful and true.

The creationist perspective is supported by many findings in space. One is the strength of planetary magnetic fields. Dr. Humphreys predicted strong magnetic fields for Uranus and Neptune, well before they were measured by the Voyager spacecraft. His predictions were accurate. Evolutionists, however, postulated that if these planets are billions of years old, their magnetic fields should be extremely weak. The strong magnetic fields of these planets suggest they are only a few thousand years old, as the Bible says.

Other examples of evidence for recent creation abound. Spiral galaxies should no longer have a spiral structure if they are literally billions of years old. Based on the rate at which they are winding themselves up now, they should be completely wound beyond recognition with no spiral arm structure visible if they were as old as is claimed.

Comets are very temporal celestial objects. Every time a comet completes an orbit in our solar system, the sun burns tons of material off the outer layers, material which then forms the tail. In other words, comets are slowly decomposing. If it were millions of years old, Halley's Comet should no longer exist. The question for evolutionists, then, is where the comets are coming from. Many of them suggest that comets are supplied by a theoretical "oort cloud." The oort cloud is purportedly a region surrounding our solar system which holds trillions of fresh comets that have never been near the sun. However, comets cannot be detected that far out in space, and there is no direct evidence that something like an oort cloud exists.[2]

According to the time frame that evolution gives for the earth-moon system, the moon would have spent the first two-thirds of its life on Earth before slowly rising into space.[3] This is based on the current rate at which the moon is moving away from the earth. This presents a problem to the evolutionary theory. The moon could not have rested on the earth intact, as the gravitational attraction between the two would have caused them to

LIGHT AND CREATION 145

> **Everyone who is seriously involved in the pursuit of science** *becomes convinced that a spirit is manifest in the laws of the universe,* **a spirit vastly superior** *to that of man, and one in the face of which we with our modest powers must* **feel humble.**
>
> ALBERT EINSTEIN

quickly assimilate into one sphere.

The point is that man's best explanation for how things could have come into existence, the Big Bang Theory, falls far short of answering all the questions. It proposes a timeline of events following the appearance of energy, but it never gets off the ground in the first place with its inability to explain how matter can arise from non-matter. Think of how incredible it would be if a scientist would somehow create something from nothing in a laboratory. But even if that would happen, the new substance would have had a cause (the scientist) that initiated it. The Big Bang, according to theory, would have had neither preexisting matter nor a cause to trigger it. The initial action of the theory can therefore be summarized as "something from nothing with nothing itself acting as a catalyst." When nothing happens to nothing, you never get everything. Zero times zero always equals zero. It is clear that God must be in the equation as the initiator of all matter and energy.

The Bible shows that the heavenly bodies were made to "be for signs, and for seasons, and for days, and years." It's interesting to note that most of our major time periods relate to the motion of objects in space. One year is precisely the amount of time the earth takes to orbit the sun. The month is based on the time span of the lunar orbit around the earth. One day is equal to one rotation of our planet. One unit of time though, the week, has no astronomical basis. It is interesting to note that even the men who reject the account of Creation are still practicing the perfect seven-day week cycle, which itself is a direct carryover from the week of Creation.

Is it illogical to believe in a Creator? Atheism says God does not exist and that it is irrational to invoke the supernatural in an explanation for the universe. But how could it be beyond the limits of reason to suggest the universe had a cause? The well-established law of cause and effect states that for every effect there is a definite cause. It is much easier to conceive a cause for the universe than to imagine that the universe came into being without pre-existing substance *and* without cause. We need not ask what caused God or where He came from, because God, being the source and embodiment of everything, is by definition a cause in Himself.

Moon

According to the Bible, time can be measured by the movement of the moon. The moon is slowly moving away from Earth, which causes a problem for the evolutionists' theory about the moon's age.

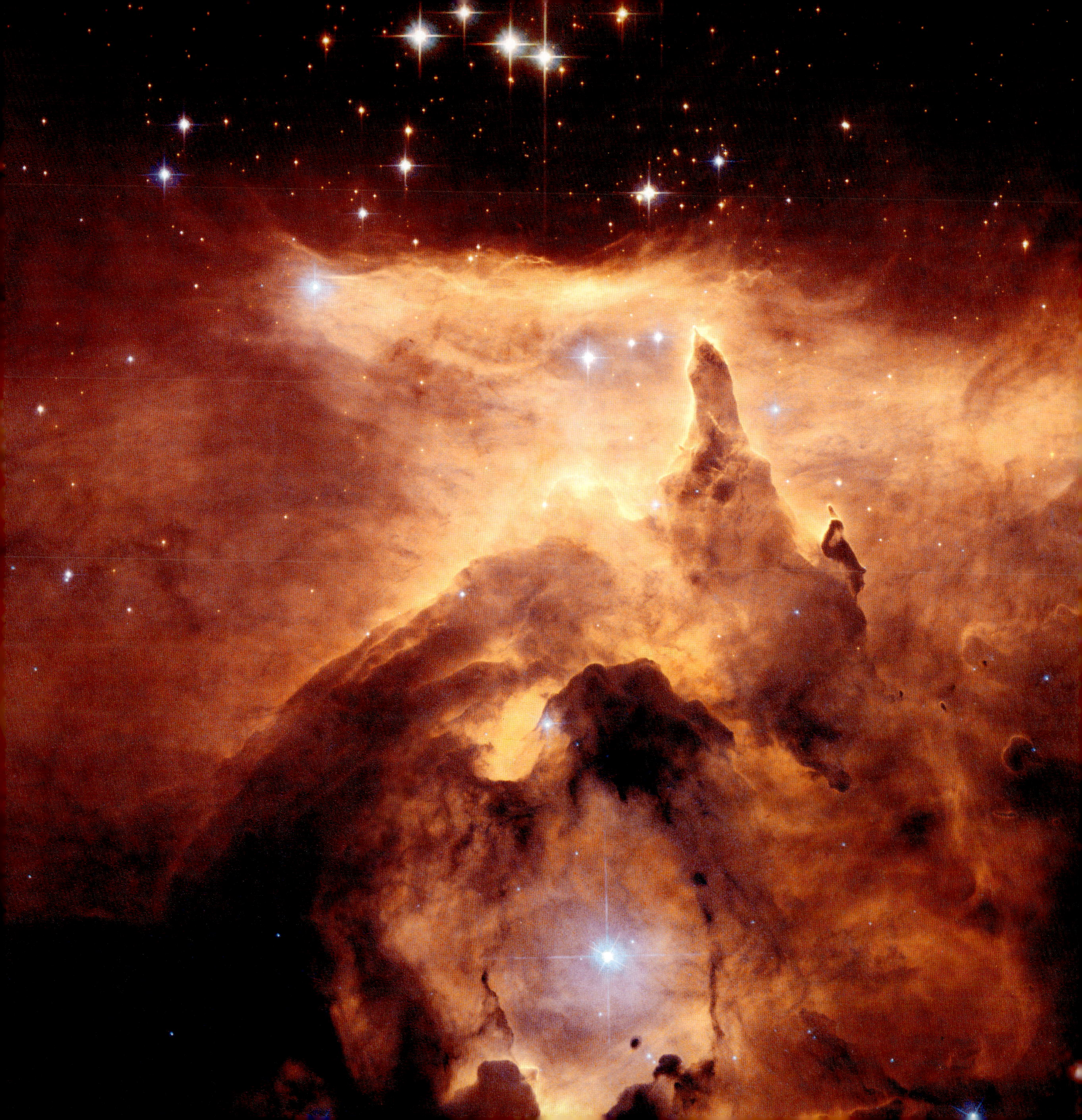

What can be more foolish than to think that all this rare fabric of heaven and earth could come by chance, *when all the skill of science is not able to make an oyster.* JEREMY TAYLOR

O magnify the LORD with me,
AND LET US EXALT HIS NAME TOGETHER.
PSALM 34:3

NGC 6357

Here a blue star sits enshrined within a glowing sphere of interstellar dust while being crowned with a sparkling cluster of stars above. It's a metaphorical picture of the tender embrace in which God holds every part of His creation.

LIGHT AND CREATION

All I have seen teaches me to
TRUST THE CREATOR FOR ALL I HAVE NOT SEEN.
RALPH WALDO EMERSON

Whirlpool Galaxy

The Whirlpool Galaxy shown here gives us one of the most impressive views of any galaxy in the universe as it displays its spiral arm design. It is located approximately 23 million light-years away.

chapter eight
The Message

We are living in a universe that is full of dynamically powerful stars with thermonuclear reactions taking place within their cores. These are spread across billions of light-years of space that's interlaced with enormous clouds of gas and dust. Along with these are **gamma ray bursts** and supernovas that emit mind-boggling amounts of energy. Scattered among them appear to be black holes that seemingly have little respect for our understanding of how things should work as they shred stars, slow the passage of time, and bend light rays. How could a universe so vast and powerful exist? We can scarcely imagine the power that first created it. The God who simply spoke the universe into existence must be unlike anything we could ever envision. Lightning that strikes 100 feet away can be a terrifying reminder of this marvelous Being's power, yet its flashes are only tiny sparks of energy from the overwhelming force that radiates from Him.

This sense of wonder culminates in a crescendo when I take a moment to look up into the expansive dome of the heavens. My depth perception and sense of distance is completely destroyed, and I am left feeling like a speck of dust swallowed up by everything, yet lost in nothingness in the middle of nowhere. Thoughts that grapple with infinity reverberate in my mind as a sense of reality deepens, revealing to me how insignificant I really am. It leaves me feeling humbled but not afraid, vulnerable yet secure, trivial yet vital, unimportant but not unloved. It's all because I realize that this mighty God imparted a portion of Himself, His life, into me when He created me, and then He made me His child. It's because I know He lost His life trying to save me—and He did this voluntarily.

Such a stupendous display of power normally has a terrifying effect on man's heart. But for the child of God, this breathtaking exhibition makes him feel safe and causes him to trust his Maker. To think that I am a part of God's family is to push my contemplation to the limit. He is my Father. His son Jesus Christ is my

For the invisible things of him from the creation of the world are clearly seen, **being understood by the things that are made, even his eternal power and Godhead; so that they are without excuse.**

ROMANS 1:20

ESO 593-8 (TOP) AND NGC 4650A (BOTTOM) Both of these galaxies resemble the cross, a symbol which represents to the Christian the most important event in history.

brother, and I will jointly inherit the kingdom with Him. And it's because HE chose to have it that way. Our God is indescribable—staggeringly marvelous and intensely wonderful on every front.

THE GALACTIC WHIRLPOOL

One of the most famous galaxies in the sky, the Whirlpool Galaxy, has been described as graceful and majestic. It is understandable why this stunning creation should be labeled with such terms. God, for some reason, has seen fit to take a so-called grand-design spiral galaxy and place it within range of high-powered photography equipment.[1] He turned its face directly toward us, giving us a dramatic view of its spectacular structure and allowing us to see the spiral arms in all of their glory. These arms are sprinkled with colorful nebulae that shimmer in their red and blue hues. As the arms spiral inward, they seem to channel our attention toward the center of the galaxy.

Astronomers were also captivated with this galaxy. They used Hubble to take the large image shown on page 150. They studied the galaxy in detail the way good scientists do when they find an excellent specimen to focus on. Then they used Hubble to zoom in on the core. When they did, they found something significant right in the center of the Whirlpool Galaxy. Massive and imposing at 100 light-years tall, this shape that resembles a cross appears tranquil and inviting, a symbol of our salvation.[2]

This, of course, is not the cross of Christ, nor do we even know that it was designed to represent it. But realizing that God formed every part of His creation to look just like it does, not accidentally but for a purpose, makes us consider that He might be trying to remind us of something. This reminder was completely hidden until modern times when, as the Bible says, men have professed themselves to be wise but have become fools. In the quest for knowledge outside of God, many men have rejected Him as Creator. They continually refuse to hear the preaching of His Word or to recognize the evidence of His creation that surrounds them on Earth. But as they lift up their hearts in search of knowledge

And I will show wonders
in heaven above. ACTS 2:19

and their own answers, they turn their scopes to the night sky, only to be shown the message once again. When we refuse to hear the message on Earth, God is faithful to show us wherever we look, even if it's 23 million light-years across the expanse of space.

THE PALE BLUE DOT

Admittedly, this photograph is not very eye-catching and is one of the least attractive in the entire book. In fact, it looks like an underexposure mistake. This image was taken by the Voyager 1 spacecraft in 1990 when it had reached the edge of the solar system. Astronomers had given it the instructions to turn around and take a series of photographs of the family of planets it had just come out of. One of the photographs that came back is displayed here. There is nothing appealing about it until we realize that the tiny blue speck of light is us. It is the earth reduced to a minute speck. If you were born before 1990, you are on this photograph! The earth and all of us put together amount to only a tiny dot. We are told in Isaiah 40:15 that "the nations are as a drop of a bucket, and are counted as the small dust of the balance." How true that is! This photo shows the earth as just a speck of dust, so fragile in appearance, suspended in a beam of sunlight.

The earth looks small because the spacecraft was so far away when the photo was taken; it had already traveled over four billion miles into space. That is a long distance, but remarkably, the spacecraft had traveled only about one-tenth of 1 percent of the way to the nearest star when it turned around and used its narrow-angle camera to catch this diminutive view of Earth. Even with this zoomed-in view, Earth was so tiny that it filled only about a tenth of a pixel on the image.

Is this how God sees us? Psalm 113:6 says of God: "Who humbleth himself to behold the things that are in heaven, and in the earth!" We look so embarrassingly small and helpless from this point of view. Every person who ever lived, from the poorest of paupers to the richest of

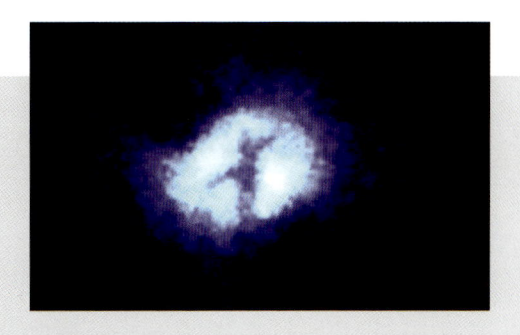

WHIRLPOOL CROSS The cross structure at the core of the Whirlpool Galaxy is likely made of galactic dust and may mark the exact position of a supermassive black hole.

PALE BLUE DOT This narrow-angle color image of the earth is a part of the first ever "portrait" of the solar system taken by Voyager 1. The spacecraft acquired a total of 60 frames for a mosaic of the solar system from a distance of more than four billion miles from Earth. From Voyager's great distance, Earth (circled) is a mere point of light, less than the size of a picture element even in the narrow-angle (high magnification) camera. Earth was a crescent only 0.12 pixel in size.

THE MESSAGE 153

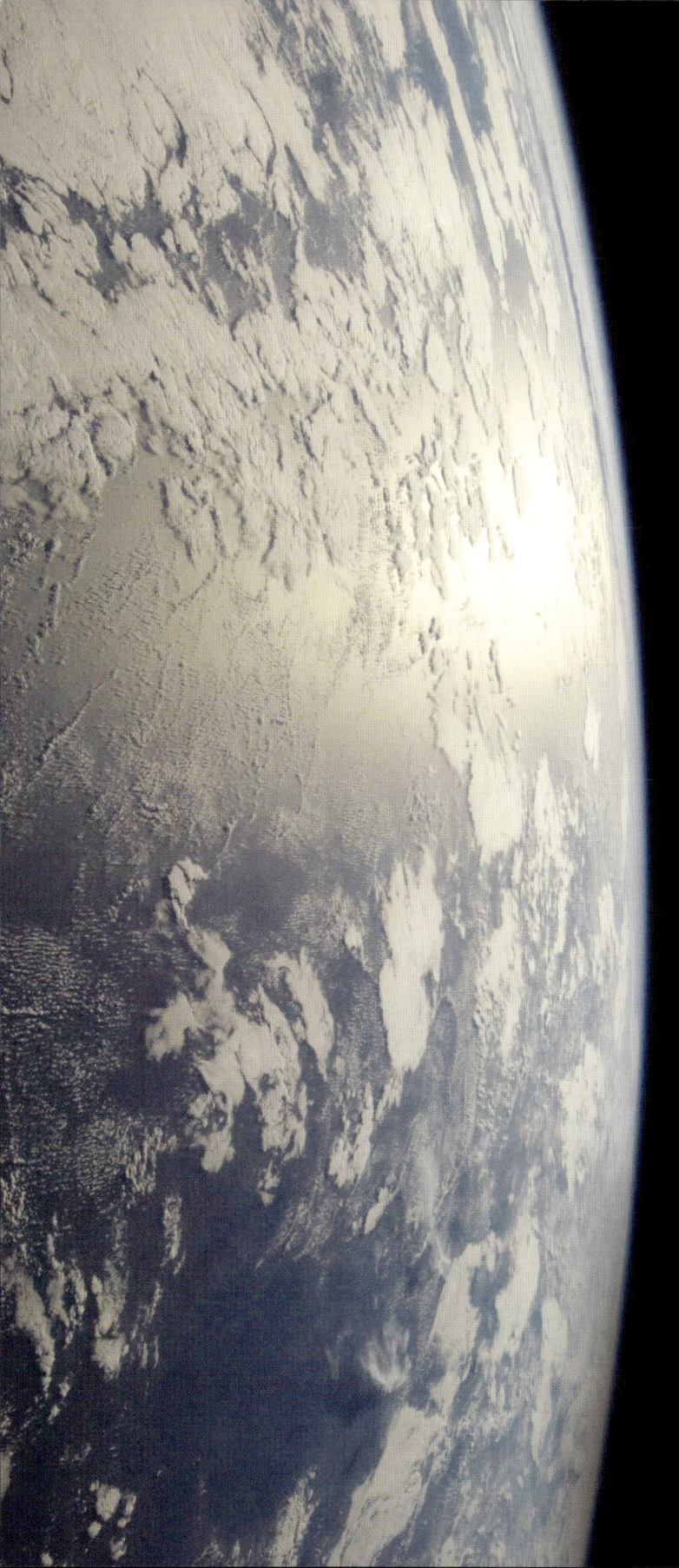

Who humbleth himself to behold the things **that are in heaven, and in the earth!**

PSALM 113:6

Earth

The earth is a vibrant oasis of life in this universe; a unique place in the cosmos that God designed with the purpose of supporting man, the unworthy pinnacle of His creation.

rulers, shared this speck of soil.

We could imagine that this is what God would see when looking in on us if He were to have normal human vision. But that would be the case only if He would first significantly reduce His greatness and move into His universe. We get the word picture in Isaiah 40:12 that God "meted out heaven with the span." A span as stated here is the width of a hand from the end of the thumb to the tip of the little finger. No one knows what the size of the universe is relative to God, but this Scripture gives the picture of God measuring out the universe with His hand. This seems to be illustrating the fact that God in His supremacy, not His physical size, is much greater than His universe.

But how would it be if we were to follow the metaphorical word picture from Isaiah 40:12 and Psalm 113:6 and imagine God with human characteristics, condescending to our low estate. What would He see? From the edge of the universe He could see, far off in the distance, the Virgo **Supercluster.** This is our area of the universe. After reducing Himself drastically again and moving into the far-flung expanse to stand outside this supercluster, He would see the cluster of galaxies we live in called the **Local Group**. As He would again make Himself vastly smaller and move into this area, He would see the Milky Way as a miniscule island universe. Lessening Himself once again to stand outside of our home galaxy, He could see far off in the distance, our stellar neighborhood. As He diminishes Himself again and moves into the vast sea of stars, He would see the tiny solar system off in the distance. With one final giant shrinking motion inward, He would arrive at the edge of the sprawling solar system where Voyager 1 drifts silently along its lonely course. Were He to have human vision, He would need to pull up His binoculars. And then, after all that, He would see, just barely, this pale blue dot.

But the amazing truth about our relationship with God is that He does not need to go to such extremes to access us. He is omnipresent! Isaiah 57:15 says, "For thus saith the high and lofty One that inhabiteth eternity, whose name is Holy; I dwell in the high and holy place, with him also that is of a contrite and humble spirit, to revive the spirit of the humble, and to revive the heart of the contrite ones." He not only dwells above us but also in the miniscule hearts of the redeemed! We are much more to Him than just insignificant specks on a pale blue dot.

Although our world is small, it is special! Life is bursting at the seams here, filling almost every space on the globe. This makes it unique. From what we can see, Earth as an oasis for life is alone in the universe. Every other place in space that we have visited was either bathed in chemicals, geologically jumbled, too cold or too hot, but *always* devoid of life. Not even the slightest glimmer of life in the form of bacteria could be found; things were completely sterile. The nearby moon is an example; its peculiar beauty comes almost entirely from its desolation. The lifeless gray dust, looming cliffs, jagged peaks, heavily cratered uplands, and lava-flooded plains all unite to form an unusual vista of alien splendor. All this—but the vibrant, throbbing pulse of life is missing.

Our world is extraordinary. It is the stage on which God introduced the pinnacle of His creation: man. Man bears the image of God Himself. Yet humans have become so lost and disoriented in the chaotic curse of sin that many are forgetting the God who made them. They flounder, searching for answers to difficult questions. Why is there pain and suffering? Why are we here? What is the purpose for life?

On Earth we do have big problems. Our problems are the result of living in a sin-cursed world. As we individually choose to live in sin, we exacerbate our problems. But many of us refuse to believe and accept that. We abuse substances that shorten lives and cause diseases. We fight against each other in wars on a global scale. Now recently we've developed nuclear weapons of mass destruction and stockpiled them in outrageous numbers. If all these weapons would continue to be stockpiled by the nations of the earth and subsequently utilized, we could very nearly end civilization as we know it. No one wants to advance in technology only to abuse it, lose control of it, and extinguish life on Earth

This photograph of the lunar terminator (boundary between dark and light) shows long shadows being cast by a tall precipice in a lava plain near the left side of the image. Near the center of the image, a mountain range extends down into the plain, ending near a well-defined crater.

The moon has a particular beauty to it, especially when seen during full moon. Up close it shows a heavily cratered scene of desolation.

in a cataclysmic nuclear apocalypse. We need answers. We need someone to save us from ourselves!

Many prominent men in our society ponder these things. If evolution is true, they theorize, then surely life would have evolved on many of the other millions of planets in space. What if we could find another civilization out in that vast expanse that began evolving millions of years before we did? If so, they would consequently have an exponential advantage over us in knowledge and technology, wouldn't they? They may have come through the terrifying times of tinkering with destructive forces much greater than themselves and survived. Perhaps they would have even found the fabled fountain of youth that allows a being to live forever. Maybe they would have developed cures for cancer, for diabetes, for heart disease—the list goes on.

As a result of such thinking, man has poured millions of dollars into the Search for Extra-Terrestrial Intelligence (SETI), a program started in 1959. A total of 42 radio telescopes are currently searching the skies. There are plans to eventually increase the number of telescopes to 350.

If only we could find extra-terrestrial intelligence in the universe around us, some fantasize, then perhaps we could locate someone who would give us hope, bring peace, and save us from ourselves and the condemnation that overshadows us with its ominous, relentless grip. Maybe we could even find someone to show us the secret to everlasting life.

Remarkably, it's not necessary to spend millions to locate this "someone." There is great news for all of mankind: our extra-terrestrial Saviour has come! He came from far outside of our civilization, down to Earth and gave us all the needed answers to our questions. He gave us the promise of the cure for all ills and gave us the true hope of eternal life. Even before we went searching for Him, He came and sought us. Not only did He share secrets with us, He was so intent on saving us from ourselves and from the pit of sin that He invested His entire life to save ours. As the blood poured down and the last

Omega Centauri

This swarm of stars, known as the globular cluster Omega Centauri, illustrates the unlimited power of God. Every star in the cluster is gigantic—sized beyond our power to comprehend.

Eye hath not seen, nor ear heard, neither have entered into the heart of man, **the things which God hath prepared for them that love him.**

1 CORINTHIANS 2:9

flicker of life wilted from His body, the immeasurable price was paid. It was finished. The very Creator of the universe, in the most astounding sacrifice of all time, had just given His invaluable life into the hands of savage men so that through the power of His death and resurrection, they could have the possibility of a glorious future they could never pay for and would in no circumstance deserve.

Yet the search goes on. SETI is searching for radio and microwave transmissions from outer space that bear a recognizable pattern of complexity, such as an intercepted TV signal, as opposed to randomness. If this is discovered, scientists agree that it means intelligence has been found. But in the highest form of irony, we are witnessing the rejection of millions of much more incredibly complex intelligent codes flooding in from every direction of the microbiological world in the form of living cells and DNA. They are rejected as the product of randomness, chance, and natural selection. Yet these are the very indicators of extra-terrestrial intelligence that scientists of our day are madly searching for. The reason for the rejection of these powerful codes is that they are the signature of an almighty and righteous God of justice. This opens up an entire new realm of profound metaphysical implications. It is hard for man to accept that a Creator exists, because this would naturally indicate that he is under ownership of that Creator and therefore accountable to Him.

The act of creation was a miracle of epic proportions that we often view too unappreciatively. Just imagine all the mass that was created at God's spoken word. Think of this: the volume of Earth could be packed into Jupiter over 1,000 times, and the volume of Jupiter could then be crammed into the sun over 1,000 times. The enormous sun is only one of billions of stars in our Milky Way Galaxy. Since it is just a **main sequence** star, the sun is dwarfed by many other stars that are much more massive, some of which could hold one billion suns inside themselves. The Milky Way Galaxy, then, is only one droplet in a sea of billions and billions of galaxies, of which we have not yet found an end.

NGC 2023

"God is light and in Him is no darkness at all." This image of NGC 2023 brings to mind the glory that is emanating from God's throne. The bright flare of light is coming from a massive star just outside the picture. It was caused by light from the star being scattered in Hubble's optical system.

THE MESSAGE

NGC 2264

This color image of the region known as NGC 2264 showcases the extraordinary beauty of the heavens. Yet this majestic nebula reflects but a small portion of the glory of our God.[a]

[a] The pillar rising from the bottom of the image is the Cone Nebula and can be seen in a close-up view on page 100.

The energy unleashed on day four of Creation, producing all the mass of the starry heavens, must have been the most frightening and phenomenal display of physical power this universe has ever witnessed. Can we even come close to imagining the staggering power of God?

Since the atomic age has dawned, we can better understand and appreciate the copious amount of energy it takes to create even a small amount of matter. The discovery that was summarized in Einstein's famous equation, $E=mc^2$, is that mass and energy are just two different manifestations of the same thing. Mass can be converted into energy, and energy can be converted back into mass. Every ounce of matter holds a tremendous amount of potential energy, and that same amount of energy was expended in the creation of it. To find the amount of energy needed to create matter, we can look at the energy capable of being released by that particular matter.

In 1945 the atomic bomb named Little Boy was dropped on Hiroshima, Japan, resulting in horrific destruction and loss of human life. The city was leveled and tens of thousands of people were killed from the initial blast. The bomb contained 141 pounds of uranium, of which only about two pounds underwent a nuclear fission reaction.[3] The sum of the matter left over from the fission reaction was only about one-thirtieth of an ounce (one gram) less than the original amount.[4] The missing matter had been explosively converted into pure energy. Only one-thirtieth of an ounce of matter had been used to obliterate the city!

The shocking message, when the process is reversed, is that in order to create a fraction of an ounce of matter, it would take the amount of energy that could destroy an entire city! What an astonishingly powerful Creator our God must be to create untold trillions of stars. We have no idea how God could have such a boundless torrent of energy issuing from Him. This powerful star-breathing, universe-upholding, supreme entity that we call Jehovah God seems so very far removed from our limited realm of time and space. Isaiah saw Him in His holy temple as cherubim flew around Him crying, "Holy, holy, holy," shielding their feet and faces from His intensely powerful glory. The temple shook with the tremendous power of God. The book of Revelation reveals that energy must be physically manifesting itself from Him because it speaks in chapter four of lightning and thunder crackling from the throne. A rainbow circles the throne as the beasts and elders fall before Him and worship.

Yet this same powerful God is a personal God and a loving Father. He accepts mere mortals as His very own and desires our time, our devotion, and our attention. He wants all of us.

How can we, laden with the scum of our sins and rebellion, ever be of such value to Him? We bear His image, and His life has been invested in us; these are two reasons why we are precious in His sight. Yet the very best actions of our own carnal selves are as filthy rags before Him. The only value we have is the value He has placed in us.

Considering the great gulf between our nature and the nature of God, it's no wonder that God condemns pride. He cannot tolerate it because of His righteous nature. James 4:6 tells us that "God resisteth the proud, but giveth grace unto the humble." The thought of the Almighty God actively working against us is too frightening to bear, but how great the contrast when He sees a humble heart and pours out the blessings of His sustaining grace!

"But will God indeed dwell on the earth? Behold, the heaven and heaven of heavens cannot contain thee" (I Kings 8:27). An affirmative answer to this question is found in Isaiah 57:15. "For thus saith the high and lofty One that inhabiteth eternity, whose name is Holy; I dwell in the high and holy place, with him also that is of a contrite and humble spirit, to revive the spirit of the humble, and to revive the heart of the contrite ones." As Psalm 139:6 says, "Such knowledge is too wonderful for me; it is high, I cannot attain unto it."

It strikes us as being somewhat strange that such a great, big, wonderful God would choose to make our bodies the dwelling place of His Spirit. One thing is certain: if He is in our hearts, it will be evident. God is far too big to be secretly stashed away in some dusty corner. If He is there, He will metaphorically "stick out everywhere." The lives of Christians should clearly show evidence of God. Sometimes it may seem convenient to hide our identity, but why would we ever have a reason to be even slightly uncomfortable to identify with Him. We serve the greatest and most powerful Being, the King of the universe! Let's unabashedly fly our flags high, declaring that we are servants of the Lord. There is no reason to ever be ashamed of Him, but if we are, He will have *plenty* of reason to be ashamed of us on Judgment Day.

It seems like a paradox that we can please such a big God with our insignificant selves, but it is true. The One who created giant spheres also delights in small things. When God wants an oak tree to grow in the backyard, He starts with an insignificant acorn.

Christ came to the earth as a helpless baby before growing into an adult and carrying out the most pivotal and important event in human history. A young boy was willing to offer His small lunch to Jesus, and 5,000 were fed from it. With God, small things can have huge ramifications.

The creation of the countless massive stars that spangle the heavens was an astounding physical display of power, but this "big" thing was rather trivial to the Creator. It was done in only one day. In the record of Creation where God details the accomplishments of that wonderful week, He summarized the overwhelming act in this underwhelming statement: "He made the stars also." The creation of the stars almost seems like an afterthought barely worth mentioning. After seemingly downplaying what seems so astonishing to us, the Bible goes on to show, in the rest of its pages, what the Creator really is concerned about. His highest joy comes from the victorious, regenerated lives of Christian believers who have a relationship with Him and are experiencing the power of the resurrection in their lives.

As God created the heavens, He plainly displayed His attributes. We can learn about the Creator by observing His celestial domain in much the same way that we can look at a house and develop a concept of the builder. A house should never get more recognition than its builder. As Hebrews 3:3 says, "He who hath builded the house hath more honour than the house." So it is with God; the glory that the heavens demonstrate all belongs to Him.

The heavens we see now are spectacular as they are, but they are marred by the curse of sin just like the rest of God's creation. As it says in 1 Corinthians 13:12, "For now we see through a glass, darkly; but then face to face." Even when we look at the heavens, it's as if we are seeing through a broken, dirty mirror—only a dim reflection of part of the glory of God. Only the most vivid imagination could come close to telling us how much more glorious the new heavens will be.

Isaiah 40:26 beckons us, "Lift up your eyes on high, and behold who hath created these things, that bringeth out their host by number: he calleth them all by names by the greatness of his might." It is saying, "Set your focus on the King; He is worthy!"

Our King takes a personal interest in every part of His creation. All the trillions and trillions of stars are individually controlled by Him. He calls them out *by name* to follow His commands. They obediently submit as they cause explosive supernovas and spectacular planetary nebulae or transform into flashing pulsars and raging black holes. Yet the same King has time for us! How much more does He care about us than the stars, since we are fashioned in His image, bought by His blood, and created to consciously praise and worship Him. This gives us tremendous value in His sight. He is so interested in every detail of our lives that He even keeps track of the number of hairs on our head.

The facts and figures about the universe can be overwhelming. We may wonder why God created such immensity. Yet this vast and awe-inspiring creation is what we can expect from a great God who is so far beyond our comprehension. His attributes reveal the same grandeur. Just as we can never expect to find the end of the universe or comprehend all of its discoveries, so we will never completely grasp the extent of the Creator's greatness or His extravagant love for us. In the midst of these mind-boggling realities, we hear the call to lives of worship. This is the invitation of our universe; this is the celestial message.

Vela Nebula

Be thou exalted, O God, **above the heavens:**
and thy glory above all the earth.

PSALM 108:5

Thou art worthy, O Lord, to receive glory and honour and power: FOR THOU HAST CREATED ALL THINGS, AND FOR THY PLEASURE THEY ARE AND WERE CREATED.

REVELATION 4:11

Centaurus A

The peculiar galaxy, Centaurus A, has a thick band of dust extending across the face of it. The image here is probably the best ever taken of this galaxy. More than 50 hours of exposure time were required to capture the image at this high level of detail and brightness.

THE MESSAGE 165

Glossary

Accretion – The process by which objects gain mass by accumulation of matter from another source.

Big Bang Theory – An explanation for the creation of the universe that assumes explosion from a single point.

Black hole – An area in space that is so dense with matter and has a gravitational field so strong that no light or any other kind of radiation or matter can escape.

Cosmic Microwave Background (CMB) – The background radiation that permeates the whole universe, believed to be radiation left over from the creation of the universe.

Cosmos – The universe as a well-ordered, harmonious system.

Cosmologists – People who study the cosmos and its history.

Electromagnetic spectrum – The complete range of all possible wavelengths of radiation which consists of periodically varying electric and magnetic fields that vibrate perpendicularly to each other and travel through space at the speed of light. Light, radio waves, and X-rays are all examples of electromagnetic radiation.

Exosphere – An envelope of very thin atmosphere surrounding a planet where the gases are gravitationally bound to the planet. The density of air is very low and the likelihood of collisions between molecules is very small.

Galaxy – A huge, gravitationally bound assemblage of stars, gas, dust, and dark matter, an example of which is our own galaxy, the Milky Way.

Gamma ray burst – A high-energy short burst of short wavelength radiation most likely originating from supernova explosions. The brightest electromagnetic source in the universe.

Giant – A category of large stars just larger than the main sequence stars.

Globular cluster – An almost spherical, compact, gravitationally-bound cluster of stars that closely orbits a galaxy.

Hypergiant – An extremely large supergiant star such as VV Cephei and VY Canis Majoris.

Hubble Space Telescope – The largest space-based optical telescope ever built. It was placed in orbit around Earth in 1990.

Inflation – A theory of faster-than-light expansion of the universe soon after the supposed occurrence of the Big Bang.

Infrared – The wavelength of light which lies just outside the visible part of the spectrum, next to the color red. It is the part of the spectrum that carries thermal energy, or heat.

Ion – An atom that has acquired an electrical charge by the addition or loss of one or more electrons.

Local Group – A group of about thirty galaxies. Our home galaxy, the Milky Way, is a part of this group.

Light-year – A unit of distance measurement equal to that traveled by a ray of light in a vacuum in one year (5.88 trillion miles).

Magnetic field – The region of space around a magnetized object where a magnetic force can be detected.

Main sequence – The most common type of star in the galaxy. The sun is included in this category.

Mass – The measure of the amount of matter an object contains, similar to weight.

Micrometeoroid – A particle of space dust. An extremely small meteoroid, typically the size of a grain of dust.

Milky Way – The name of our home galaxy. It can be seen at night as a faint milky glow extending from the northern to the southern horizon on a clear, moonless night.

Nebula (plural **Nebulae**) – A large cloud-like region in space where gases and dust are distributed in varying patterns. These can be illuminated or dark.

Nuclear fusion – A situation in which two or more atomic nuclei collide at high speed and combine to form a new type of heavier atomic nucleus. Not all of the mass from the original nuclei is conserved in this process, but some is converted into a large amount of energy such as heat and light.

Open star cluster – A loosely arranged cluster of stars within a galaxy.

Planet – Large, non-stellar object orbiting the sun or another star and shining only by reflected light.

Plasma – Almost completely ionized gas that has been superheated beyond the normal gaseous state.

Pulsar – A rapidly spinning neutron star (extremely compacted star whose density equals that of a neutron), emitting two beams of radio waves that are seen on Earth as pulses.

Quasar –The highly energetic center of an active galaxy. The most powerful continuously shining object known.

Solar system – The collective name given to the sun and all the celestial bodies within its gravitational influence.

Stellar – Pertaining to stars.

Sunspot – A temporary concentration of strong magnetic fields detected as a darkened area in the white light of the sun's photosphere.

Supercluster – An extensive collection of galaxies made up of smaller galaxy clusters.

Supergiant – The largest and most luminous star(s) known. The largest stars within this category are called hypergiants.

Supernova – A stellar explosion that involves the disruption and dispersion of virtually an entire star.

Image Credits

Introductory Pages

Pages ii and iii: G.Miley and R. Overzier (Leiden Observatory), and the ACS Science Team

Pages iv and v: © Ken Crawford, www.imagingdeepsky.com, used by permission.

Page vi: ESO/Igor Chekalin

Pages viii and ix: Created by Andrew Z Colvin, Modified by Morris Yoder

Chapter One

Page 10: ESO/J. Emerson/VISTA. Acknowledgment: Cambridge Astronomical Survey Unit

Page 13: NASA, ESA, and the Hubble Heritage Team (STScI/AURA). *Caption by NASA.*

Pages 14 and 15: ESO/S. Guisard (www.eso.org/~sguisard)

Pages 18 and 19: ESO/T. Preibisch

Chapter Two

Page 20: ESA/Hubble & NASA

Page 22: ESA/NASA/SOHO. *Caption by NASA.*

Page 23: NASA/SDO and the AIA, EVE, and HMI science teams. *Caption by NASA.*

Page 24: NASA/SDO and the AIA, EVE, and HMI science teams

Page 25: NASA/SDO and the AIA, EVE, and HMI science teams. *Caption by NASA.*

Page 26: NASA/SDO and the AIA, EVE, and HMI science teams. *Caption by NASA.*

Page 27: Photo by Joshua Strang. Used by permission of US Air Force.

Page 28: SOHO (ESA & NASA). *Caption by NASA.*

Page 29 (left): NASA/SDO and the AIA, EVE, and HMI science teams

Page 29 (right): NASA/SDO and the AIA, EVE, and HMI science teams. *Caption by NASA.*

Page 30: NASA, ESA, and the Hubble Heritage Team (STScI/AURA). *Caption by NASA.*

Pages 32 and 33: Adam Evans

Page 34: Morris Yoder

Pages 36 and 37: NASA, ESA, the Hubble Heritage Team (STScI/AURA), and R. Gendler (for the Hubble Heritage Team). Acknowledgment: J. GaBany.

Page 38: Images compiled by Morris Yoder

Page 39: Images compiled by Morris Yoder

Page 40: Images compiled by Morris Yoder

Page 41 (top): NASA, ESA, and R. Humphreys (University of Minnesota). *Caption by NASA.*

Page 41 (bottom): Public Domain (Wikipedia User Mysid)

Page 42: The Hubble Heritage Team (AURA/STScI/NASA). *Caption by NASA.*

Page 43 (top): NASA/SDO and the AIA, EVE, and HMI science teams. *Caption by NASA.*

Page 43 (bottom): NASA/SDO and the AIA, EVE, and HMI science teams. *Caption by NASA.*

Page 44: NASA and Don F. Figer (UCLA). *Caption by NASA.*

Page 45 (top): NASA/JPL-Caltech. *Caption by NASA.*

Page 45 (bottom): NASA and The Hubble Heritage Team (STScI/AURA). *Caption by NASA.*

Page 46 (top): L. Ferrarese (Johns Hopkins University) and NASA. *Caption by NASA.*

Page 46 (bottom): NASA/Dana Berry/SkyWorks Digital. *Caption by NASA.*

Page 47: NASA, ESA, J. Hester and A. Loll (Arizona State University). *Caption by NASA.*

Page 48: NASA/HST/CXC/ASU/J. Hester et al. *Caption by NASA.*

Page 49 (top): NASA, ESA, K. France (University of Colordo, Boulder), and P. Challis and R. Kirshner (Harvard-Smithsonian Center for Astrophysics). *Caption by NASA.*

Page 49 (middle): NASA and J. Morse (University of Colorado). *Caption by NASA.*

Page 49 (bottom): X-ray: NASA/CXC/SAO/J.Hughes et al, Optical: NASA/ESA/Hubble Heritage Team (STScI/AURA)
Page 50: NASA, ESA, and the Hubble Heritage Team (STScI/AURA). *Caption by NASA.*

Chapter Three
Page 52: NASA/JPL. *Caption by NASA.*
Page 54: NASA/Johns Hopkins University Applied Physics Laboratory/Carnegie Institution of Washington. *Caption by NASA.*
Page 55: NASA/Johns Hopkins University Applied Physics Laboratory/Southwest Research Institute/GSFC. *Caption by NASA.*
Page 56: NASA/JPL
Page 57: ESA/ J. Whatmore
Page 58 (top): NSSDC, NASA
Page 58 (bottom): JAXA/NASA/Lockheed Martin
Page 59: NASA/JPL/USGS
Page 60: NASA/JPL-Caltech/University of Arizona
Page 61 (top): NASA/JPL/University of Arizona
Page 61 (upper middle): NASA/JPL-Caltech/University of Arizona
Page 61 (lower middle): NASA/JPL-Caltech/University of Arizona. *Caption by NASA.*
Page 61 (bottom): NASA/JPL-Caltech/University of Arizona. *Caption by NASA.*
Page 62: NASA/JPL/University of Arizona. *Caption by NASA.*
Page 63 (top): NASA, ESA, and H. Weaver and E. Smith (STScI)
Page 63 (bottom left): NASA/JPL
Page 63 (bottom right): R. Evans, J. Trauger, H. Hammel and the HST Comet Science Team and NA
Page 65: NASA/JPL/Space Science Institute. *Caption by NASA.*
Page 66 (top left): NASA/JPL/Space Science Institute
Page 66 (top right): NASA, ESA, J. Clarke (Boston University), and Z. Levay (STScI)
Pages 66 and 67 (bottom): NASA/JPL
Page 67 (top left): NASA/JPL/Space Science Institute
Page 67 (top right): NASA/JPL/Space Science Institute
Page 68 (top left): NASA/JPL-Caltech/Space Science Institute
Page 68 (top right): NASA/JPL/Space Science Institute
Page 68 (middle): NASA/JPL/Space Science Institute. *Caption by NASA.*
Page 68 (bottom): NASA/JPL-Caltech/Space Science Institute. *Caption by NASA.*
Page 69: NASA/JPL/Voyager mission
Page 70 (top): NASA/JPL
Page 70 (bottom): NASA/JPL
Page 71: Calvin J. Hamilton, used by permission.

Chapter Four
Page 72: NASA, ESA, and the Hubble Heritage (STScI/AURA)-ESA/Hubble Collaboration; Acknowledgment: R. Chandar (University of Toledo) and J. Miller (University of Michigan). *Caption by NASA.*
Page 74: NASA and The Hubble Heritage Team (STScI/AURA); Acknowledgment: Ray A. Lucas (STScI/AURA). *Caption by NASA.*
Page 75: NASA, ESA, A. Riess (STScI/JHU), L. Macri (Texas A & M University), and the Hubble Heritage Team (STScI/AURA). *Caption by NASA.*
Page 76: NASA, ESA, and The Hubble Heritage Team (STScI/AURA). *Caption by NASA.*
Page 77: NASA, ESA, and The Hubble Heritage Team (STScI/AURA); Acknowledgment: J. Gallagher (University of Wisconsin), M. Mountain (STScI), and P. Puxley (National Science Foundation). *Caption by NASA.*
Page 78: ESA/Hubble & NASA. *Caption by NASA.*
Page 79: NASA, ESA, and the Hubble Heritage (STScI/AURA)-ESA/Hubble Collaboration; Acknowledgment: A. Fabian (Institute of Astronomy, University of Cambridge, UK). *Caption by NASA.*
Page 80: NASA, ESA, and The Hubble Heritage Team (STScI/AURA); Acknowledgment: P. Knezek (WIYN)
Page 81: NASA, ESA, and The Hubble Heritage Team (STScI/AURA); Acknowledgment: P. Goudfrooij (STScI). *Caption by NASA.*
Page 82: NASA, ESA, and the Hubble Heritage (STScI/AURA)-ESA/Hubble Collaboration; Acknowledgment: M. Crockett and S. Kaviraj (Oxford University, UK), R. O'Connell (University of Virginia), B. Whitmore (STScI), and the WFC3 Scientific Oversight Committee
Page 83: NASA, ESA and W. Harris (McMaster University, Ontario, Canada)

Page 84: NASA and The Hubble Heritage Team (STScI/AURA). *Caption by NASA.*
Page 85: NASA, H. Ford (JHU), G. Illingworth (UCSC/LO), M.Clampin (STScI), G. Hartig (STScI), the ACS Science Team, and ESA
Page 86: NASA, H. Ford (JHU), G. Illingworth (UCSC/LO), M.Clampin (STScI), G. Hartig (STScI), the ACS Science Team, and ESA. *Caption by NASA.*
Page 89: NASA, ESA, and the Hubble Heritage Team (STScI/AURA)
Page 91: NASA, ESA, and S. Beckwith (STScI) and the HUDF Team. *Caption by NASA.*

Chapter Five
Page 92: NASA,ESA, M. Robberto (Space Telescope Science Institute/ESA) and the Hubble Space Telescope Orion Treasury Project Team. *Caption by NASA.*
Pages 94 and 95: T. A. Rector & B. A. Wolpa, NOAO, AURA, used by permission. Copyright Information: http://www.noao.edu/image_gallery/copyright.html.
Pages 96 and 97: NASA, ESA, STScI, J. Hester and P. Scowen (Arizona State University)
Pages 98 and 99: NASA, ESA, and The Hubble Heritage Team (STScI/AURA)
Page 100: NASA, H. Ford (JHU), G. Illingworth (UCSC/LO), M.Clampin (STScI), G. Hartig (STScI), the ACS Science Team, and ESA. *Caption by NASA.*
Page 102: NASA, ESA, N. Smith (University of California, Berkeley), and The Hubble Heritage Team (STScI/AURA)
Page 103 (background): ESA/Hubble & NASA
Page 103 (inset): A. Caulet (ST-ECF, ESA) and NASA
Page 104: NASA, The Hubble Heritage Team (AURA/STScI). *Caption by NASA.*
Page 105: NASA, ESA, and M. Livio and the Hubble 20th Anniversary Team (STScI). *Caption by NASA.*
Page 107: © Ken Crawford, www.imagingdeepsky.com, used by permission.
Page 109: NASA, ESA, and the Hubble Heritage Team (STScI/AURA). *Caption by NASA.*
Page 110: NASA, ESA and J. Hester (ASU). *Caption by NASA.*

Page 111: NASA, ESA and A. Nota (STScI/ESA)
Pages 112 and 113: NASA, ESA, D. Lennon and E. Sabbi (ESA/STScI), J. Anderson, S. E. de Mink, R. van der Marel, T. Sohn, and N. Walborn (STScI), N. Bastian (Excellence Cluster, Munich), L. Bedin (INAF, Padua), E. Bressert (ESO), P. Crowther (University of Sheffield), A. de Koter (University of Amsterdam), C. Evans (UKATC/STFC, Edinburgh), A. Herrero (IAC, Tenerife), N. Langer (AifA, Bonn), I. Platais (JHU), and H. Sana (University of Amsterdam). *Caption by NASA.*
Pages 114 and 115: NASA, ESA, N. Smith (University of California, Berkeley), and The Hubble Heritage Team (STScI/AURA)
Page 116: ESO
Page 117: NASA and Jeff Hester (Arizona State University). *Caption by NASA.*
Page 118 (left): NASA, NOAO, ESA, the Hubble Helix Nebula Team, M. Meixner (STScI), and T.A. Rector (NRAO).
Page 118 (right): C. Robert O'Dell and Kerry P. Handron (Rice University), NASA
Page 119: NASA, NOAO, ESA, the Hubble Helix Nebula Team, M. Meixner (STScI), and T.A. Rector (NRAO). *Caption by NASA.*
Page 120 (top): NASA, ESA, HEIC, and The Hubble Heritage Team (STScI/AURA). *Caption by NASA.*
Page 120 (bottom): NASA, Andrew Fruchter and the ERO Team [Sylvia Baggett (STScI), Richard Hook (ST-ECF), Zoltan Levay (STScI)]. *Caption by NASA.*
Page 121: © Ken Crawford, www.imagingdeepsky.com, used by permission.
Page 122 (top): Raghvendra Sahai and John Trauger (JPL), the WFPC2 science team, and NASA
Page 122 (middle): Bruce Balick (University of Washington), Vincent Icke (Leiden University, The Netherlands), Garrelt Mellema (Stockholm University), and NASA. *Caption by NASA.*
Page 122 (bottom): NASA; ESA; Hans Van Winckel (Catholic University of Leuven, Belgium); and Martin Cohen (University of California, Berkeley)

Page 123: NASA, ESA, and the Hubble SM4 ERO Team. *Caption by NASA.*

Page 124 (top): NASA and The Hubble Heritage Team (AURA/STScI)

Page 124 (middle): The Hubble Heritage Team (STScI/AURA/NASA)

Page 124 (bottom): NASA, ESA, and K. Noll (STScI). *Caption by NASA.*

Page 125: NASA, ESA, and the Hubble Heritage Team (STScI/AURA). *Caption by NASA.*

Page 126: NASA and The Hubble Heritage Team (STScI/AURA). *Caption by NASA.*

Page 127: Hubble Heritage Team (AURA/STScI/NASA/ESA)

Pages 128 and 129: NASA, ESA, and the Hubble Heritage Team (STScI/AURA)

Page 130: NASA and the Hubble Heritage Team (AURA/STScI). *Caption by NASA.*

Page 131: NASA, ESA and H.E. Bond (STScI)

Chapter Six

Page 132: NASA/ESA

Page 135: Digitized Sky Survey, ESA/ESO/NASA FITS Liberator. *Caption by NASA.*

Page 136: NASA, ESA and AURA/Caltech. *Caption by NASA.*

Page 137: NASA, STScI. *Caption by NASA.*

Chapter Seven

Page 138: NASA/JPL-Caltech/UCLA. *Caption by NASA.*

Page 140: NASA. Adapted by Wikimedia user "Inductiveload."

Page 141: NASA, ESA, S. Baum and C. O'Dea (RIT), R. Perley and W. Cotton (NRAO/AUI/NSF), and the Hubble Heritage Team (STScI/AURA). *Caption by NASA.*

Page 142: NASA, ESA, and R. Humphreys (University of Minnesota)

Page 144: NASA, ESA, the Hubble Heritage (STScI/AURA)-ESA/Hubble Collaboration, and W. Keel (University of Alabama, Tuscaloosa)

Page 147: Morris Yoder

Page 148: NASA, ESA, and J. Maíz Apellániz (Instituto de Astrofísica de Andalucía, Spain)

Chapter Eight

Page 150: NASA, ESA, S. Beckwith (STScI), and The Hubble Heritage Team (STScI/AURA)

Page 152 (top): NASA, ESA, the Hubble Heritage (STScI/AURA)-ESA/Hubble Collaboration, and A. Evans (University of Virginia, Charlottesville/NRAO/Stony Brook University)

Page 152 (bottom): The Hubble Heritage Team (AURA/STScI/NASA)

Page 153 (top): H. Ford (JHU/STScI), the Faint Object Spectrograph IDT, and NASA

Page 153 (bottom): NASA/JPL. *Caption by NASA.*

Page 154: Image Science & Analysis Laboratory, NASA Johnson Space Center

Page 156 (top): Morris Yoder

Page 156 (bottom): Morris Yoder

Page 157: ESO/INAF-VST/OmegaCAM. Acknowledgement: A. Grado/INAF-Capodimonte Observatory

Page 158: ESA/Hubble & NASA

Page 160: ESO

Page 163: © Robert Gendler, www.robgendlerastropics.com, used by permission.

Pages 164 and 165: ESO

Page 174: ESA/Hubble

End Notes

Chapter One

[1] Maurice Thaddeus Brackbill, *The Heavens Declare*, (Chicago: Moody Bible Institute & Bookmark Publishing, 1959), p. 129.
[2] Ray Comfort, *Scientific Facts in the Bible*, (Orlando, FL: Bridge-Logos, 2001), p. 11.
[3] Ibid., p. 14.
[4] Ibid., p. 13.

Chapter Two

[1] Maurice Thaddeus Brackbill, *The Heavens Declare*, (Chicago: Moody Bible Institute & Bookmark Publishing, 1959), p. 51.
[2] "Tiny Nukes, *Popular Mechanics*, October 2002, p. 69.
[3] Maurice Thaddeus Brackbill, *The Heavens Declare*, (Chicago: Moody Bible Institute & Bookmark Publishing, 1959), p. 50.
[4] Dr. Tony Phillips, "New Solar Cycle Prediction," May 29, 2009, <http://science.nasa.gov/science-news/science-at-nasa/2009/29may_noaaprediction/>, accessed on February 12, 2013.
[5] Jeff Scott, "Spacecraft Speed Records," February 5, 2006, <http://www.aerospaceweb.org/question/spacecraft/q0260.shtml>, accessed on March 1, 2013.
[6] Dr. Louis Barbier, "How Much Energy Does the Sun Produce?" <http://helios.gsfc.nasa.gov/qa_sun.html#power>, accessed on October 15, 2012.
[7] "Hubble Identifies What May Be the Most Luminous Star Known," October 8, 1997, <http://hubblesite.org/newscenter/archive/releases/1997/33>, accessed on October 15, 2012.
[8] Terence Dickinson, *The Universe and Beyond*, 4th ed., (Buffalo, NY: Firefly Books, 2004), p. 112.
[9] The Star Child Team/NASA, "Quasars," <http://starchild.gsfc.nasa.gov/docs/StarChild/universe_level2/quasars.html>, accessed on January 3, 2013.

[10] "Crab Nebula," *Oxford Astronomy Encyclopedia*, 2002, p. 104.
[11] Bill Steigerwald, "Potential New NASA Mission Would Reveal the Hearts of Undead Stars," November, 9, 2011, <http://www.nasa.gov/topics/universe/features/nicer-science.html>, accessed on November 12, 2012.

Chapter Three

[1] "NASA Solar System Exploration: Mercury: Read More," <http://solarsystem.nasa.gov/planets/profile.cfm?Object=Mercury&Display=OverviewLong>, accessed on November 12, 2012.
[2] Ibid.
[3] Ibid.
[4] Ibid.
[5] "NASA Solar System Exploration: Venus: Read More," <http://solarsystem.nasa.gov/planets/profile.cfm?Object=Venus&Display=OverviewLong>, accessed on November 13, 2012.
[6] "Venus," *Oxford Astronomy Encyclopedia*, 2002, p.429.
[7] "Venus," *Oxford Astronomy Encyclopedia*, 2002, p.429.
[8] "NASA Solar System: "Mars: Read More," <http://solarsystem.nasa.gov/planets/profile.cfm?Object=Mars&Display=OverviewLong>, accessed on November 15, 2012.
[9] "NASA Solar System: Jupiter, Facts and Figures," <http://solarsystem.nasa.gov/planets/profile.cfm?Object=Jupiter&Display=Facts>, accessed on November 15, 2012.
[10] Ibid.
[11] "NASA Solar System: Saturn: Read More," <http://solarsystem.nasa.gov/planets/profile.cfm?Object=Saturn&Display=OverviewLong>, accessed on November 18, 2012.
[12] William B. Hubbard et al., "Saturn," *Encyclopedia Britannica* Online Academic Edition, Encyclopedia Britannica Inc., March 6, 2013, <http://www.britannica.com/EBchecked/topic/525169/Saturn/54280/The-interior>, accessed on February 25, 2013.
[13] "NASA Solar System: Saturn: Read More," <http://solarsystem.nasa.gov/planets/profile.cfm?Object=Saturn&Display=OverviewLong>, accessed on March 1, 2013.
[14] "NASA Solar System: Uranus: Read More," <http://

solarsystem.nasa.gov/planets/profile.cfm?Object=Uranus&Display=OverviewLong>, accessed on November 19, 2012.

[15]"NASA Solar System: Neptune: Read More," <http://solarsystem.nasa.gov/planets/profile.cfm?Object=Neptune&Display=OverviewLong>, accessed on November 19, 2012.

[16]Ibid.

Chapter Four

[1]Terence Dickinson, *The Universe and Beyond*, 4th ed., (Buffalo, NY: Firefly Books, 2004), p. 133.

[2]"Hubble's Deepest View Ever of the Universe Unveils Earliest Galaxies," March 9, 2004, <hubblesite.org/newscenter/archive/releases/2004/07/>, accessed on December 11, 2012.

[3]Ibid.

[4]Terence Dickinson, *The Universe and Beyond*, 4th ed., (Buffalo, NY: Firefly Books, 2004), p. 133.

Chapter Five

[1]"Hubble Finds Thousands of Gaseous Fragments Surrounding a Dying Star," April 15, 1996, <hubblesite.org/newscenter/archive/releases/1996/13/image/a>, accessed on October 20, 2012.

Chapter Six

[1]Lars Lindberg Christensen and Robert A. Fosbury, *Hubble: 15 Years of Discovery,* (New York: Springer, 2006), p. 14.

Chapter Seven

[1]Dr. Jason Lisle, *Taking Back Astronomy*, (Green Forest, AR: Master Books, 2006), pp. 48-50.

[2]Ibid., p. 68.

[3]Ibid., p. 55.

Chapter Eight

[1]K. Takáts and J. Vinkó, "Distance estimate and progenitor characteristics of SN 2005cs in M51," November 2006, <http://articles.adsabs.harvard.edu/cgi-bin/nph-iarticle_query?2006MNRAS.372.1735T&data_type=PDF_HIGH&whole_paper=YES&type=PRINTER&filetype=.pdf>, accessed on October 20, 2012.

[2]"NASA's Hubble Space Telescope Resolves a Dark "x" Across the Nucleus of M51," June 8, 1992, <http://hubblesite.org/newcenter/archive/releases/1992/17/image/a/>, accessed on October 20, 2012.

[3]Samuel Glasstone and Philip J. Dolan, *The Effects of Nuclear Weapons* (Department of Defense), pp. 12-13; qtd on "Little Boy," <http://en.wikipedia.org/wiki/Little_Boy>, accessed on December 20, 2012.

[4]"Little Boy" <http://www.mashpedia.com/Little_Boy>, accessed on December 19, 2012.

If you cannot accept a Saviour, NEITHER CAN YOU AFFORD A CREATOR.

About the Author

Morris Yoder is a lifelong resident of Montezuma, Georgia. His fascination with the heavenly realm was born out of tragedy. As a five-year-old boy, he and his mother rushed to the family farm after hearing that his father had been attacked by a bull. There, Morris saw his badly wounded father, Allen, barely clinging to consciousness. A few hours later he passed away.

Morris remembers that his life was instantly changed by this event. An ominous, foreboding sense of emptiness held him in its clutch. In his childlike way of thinking, he couldn't understand why a good God would let a bad bull kill his father. As a result, he became bitter, lonely, and withdrawn.

Through this period of his life, Morris's mother remained consistent in her love and nurture. As he grew older, Morris heard testimonies about how God was working in the lives of others. He felt tired of resenting God and wanted to experience His goodness too. In addition, he desperately wanted a father figure in his life. So, several years after his father's death, Morris made a pact with God. He told God that he would accept what had happened to his father, if God would fill the emptiness in his life and be a personal father to him. God responded to that prayer, and in the years that followed, He revealed Himself to Morris so clearly that it seemed God was always with him just as his earthly father had been.

As Morris looked up into the sky on quiet nights, the awe-inspiring heavens helped to soothe the gloomy emptiness in his being by speaking of something far greater than anything he had experienced on earth. He felt certain as he gazed upward that he was seeing the place where his father had gone and where his new Father dwelled. These realizations sparked his keen interest in the heavens and ultimately led to a more serious study of the cosmos.

In recent years, Morris has been sharing his findings with others at churches and community events. He is also a regular writer for the children's magazine, Nature Friend.

Morris has been married to his wife Elizabeth since 2010. They have one son, Allen. Morris enjoys hearing from his readers and can be contacted at morrisayoder@yahoo.com. You may also write to him in care of Christian Aid Ministries, P.O. Box 360, Berlin, Ohio 44610.

Christian Aid Ministries

Christian Aid Ministries was founded in 1981 as a nonprofit, tax-exempt 501(c)(3) organization. Its primary purpose is to provide a trustworthy and efficient channel for Amish, Mennonite, and other conservative Anabaptist groups and individuals to minister to physical and spiritual needs around the world. This is in response to the command ". . . do good unto all men, especially unto them who are of the household of faith" (Gal. 6:10).

Each year, CAM supporters provide approximately 15 million pounds of food, clothing, medicines, seeds, Bibles, Bible story books, and other Christian literature for needy people. Most of the aid goes to orphans and Christian families. Supporters' funds also help clean up and rebuild for natural disaster victims, put up Gospel billboards in the U.S., support several church-planting efforts, operate two medical clinics, and provide resources for needy families to make their own living. CAM's main purposes for providing aid are to help and encourage God's people and to bring the Gospel to a lost and dying world.

CAM has staff, warehouse, and distribution networks in Romania, Moldova, Ukraine, Haiti, Nicaragua, Liberia, and Israel. Aside from management, supervisory personnel, and bookkeeping operations, volunteers do most of the work at CAM locations. Each year, volunteers at our warehouses, field bases, DRS projects, and other locations donate over 200,000 hours of work.

CAM's ultimate purpose is to glorify God and help enlarge His kingdom. ". . . whatsoever ye do, do all to the glory of God" (1 Cor. 10:31).

The Way to God and Peace

We live in a world contaminated by sin. Sin is anything that goes against God's holy standards. When we do not follow the guidelines that God our Creator gave us, we are guilty of sin. Sin separates us from God, the source of life.

Since the time when the first man and woman, Adam and Eve, sinned in the Garden of Eden, sin has been universal. The Bible says that we all have "sinned and come short of the glory of God" (Romans 3:23). It also says that the natural consequence for that sin is eternal death, or punishment in an eternal hell: "Then when lust hath conceived, it bringeth forth sin: and sin, when it is finished, bringeth forth death" (James 1:15).

But we do not have to suffer eternal death in hell. God provided forgiveness for our sins through the death of His only Son, Jesus Christ. Because Jesus was perfect and without sin, He could die in our place. "For God so loved the world that he gave his only begotten Son, that whosoever believeth in him should not perish, but have everlasting life" (John 3:16).

A sacrifice is something given to benefit someone else. It costs the giver greatly. Jesus was God's sacrifice. Jesus' death takes away the penalty of sin for everyone who accepts this sacrifice and truly repents of their sins. To repent of sins means to be truly sorry for and turn away from the things we have done that have violated God's standards (Acts 2:38; 3:19).

Jesus died, but He did not remain dead. After three days, God's Spirit miraculously raised Him to life again. God's Spirit does something similar in us. When we receive Jesus as our sacrifice and repent of our sins, our hearts are changed. We become spiritually alive! We develop new desires and attitudes (2 Corinthians 5:17). We begin to make choices that please God (1 John 3:9). If we do fail and commit sins, we can ask God for forgiveness. "If we confess our sins, he is faithful and just to forgive us our sins, and to cleanse us from all unrighteousness" (1 John 1:9).

Once our hearts have been changed, we want to continue growing spiritually. We will be happy to let Jesus be the Master of our lives and will want to become more like Him. To do this, we must meditate on God's Word and commune with God in prayer. We will testify to others of this change by being baptized and sharing the good news of God's victory over sin and death. Fellowship with a faithful group of believers will strengthen our walk with God (1 John 1:7).

Index

A
accretion disk 44
Alnilam 135
Alnitak 135
Andromeda Galaxy 11, 33, 35
Arcturus 38–40
asteroids VII, 28, 55, 62, 90

B
Betelgeuse VII, 38–40
Big Bang Theory 143, 145–146
black holes 44–46, 140, 151, 153, 162
Brahe, Tycho 12
Bubble Nebula 121
Butterfly Nebula 123

C
Caloris Basin 55
Carina Nebula 95, 102, 104–105, 115
Cassini 62, 64, 66–68
Caterpillar 115
Cat's Eye Nebula 120
Centaurus A (galaxy) 165
cometary knots 118
comets VII, 28, 62–63, 118, 120, 145
Cone Nebula 101, 160
Copernicus, Nicolaus 16
Cosmic Microwave Background 143
cosmos VII, 15, 17, 45, 73, 91, 132, 143, 154
Crab Nebula 45–47
Crab Pulsar 46, 48–49

D
Dione 67–68
dust devils 58, 61

E
Eagle Nebula 95–96, 98
Earth 11, 21, 24–25, 27–28, 33, 41–42, 44–46, 53, 55, 57–58, 60, 62–64, 66, 68–72, 75–76, 84, 93, 96, 102, 115, 117–118, 122–123, 126, 132–134, 139, 142–143, 145–147, 152–153, 156, 159, 161–162
  deterioration 16
  distance from sun 31
  oasis of life 154–155
  pale blue dot 66, 153, 155
  rotation 16
  size compared VII, 12, 29, 38, 40
electromagnetic spectrum 140
Eskimo Nebula 120
ESO 593-8 152
Eta Carinae 49
Europa 62
evolutionary theory 16, 70, 145
exosphere 55
eyes
  adapting to the dark 133
  best tool 133

F
Flame Nebula 135

G
galaxy VII, 11–12, 15, 31, 33, 35, 40, 42, 44–46, 49–50, 72, 73–91, 111, 113, 118, 133, 137, 140, 145, 150, 152, 155, 159, 165
  spiral 72, 75, 78, 80, 82, 84, 87, 145, 150, 152
gamma ray bursts 151
globular cluster 31, 45, 157
Great Dark Spot 70–71
Great Red Spot 63–64

H
Halley's Comet 145
HD 44179 (nebula) 122
helium 21, 46
Helix Nebula 118, 119
Hellas Planitia 60
Hercules A 140
Hoag's Object 74
Horsehead Nebula 106, 135
Hourglass Nebula 118, 122
Hubble Space Telescope 13, 45–46, 49, 74–76, 79, 84, 90–91, 105, 113, 122, 124, 130, 132, 134
hydrogen 21, 41, 46, 72, 77, 110

I
inflation model 143
ions 55

J
Jupiter 35, 38, 40, 53, 62–64, 159

K
Kepler, Johannes 12
Keyhole Nebula 104

L
Lagoon Nebula 103
Large Magellanic Cloud 113
light
  properties of 139
  speed of 139

light-year, definition 35
lunar terminator 156

M

M2-9 (nebula) 122
M17 *See* Omega Nebula
M54 (globular cluster) 20
M80 (globular cluster) 42
M81 (galaxy) 76
M82 (galaxy) 77
M87 (galaxy) 45
M100 (galaxy) 137
magnetic field 21, 25, 43, 79, 145
magnetosphere 25, 55, 67
Mars 40, 53, 58–61
Mercury 40, 53–55, 57
Messier 74 (galaxy) 72
Messier 104 (galaxy) 84
microwaves 139
Milky Way Galaxy VII, 11, 15, 31, 33, 35, 73, 159
Mimas 67
Mintaka 135
moon 28, 31, 35, 46, 62–63, 68, 71, 76, 88, 93, 101, 123, 139, 145, 147, 155–156
Mystic Mountain 105

N

Nebulae VII, 93
   emission 93, 106
   planetary 13, 90, 118–120, 122, 124, 126–127, 162
   reflection 93
Neptune 40, 69–71, 145
Neutron stars, *See* stars, pulsars
NGC 602 (nebula) 108
NGC 634 (galaxy) 78
NGC 1275 (galaxy) 79
NGC 1300 (galaxy) 80
NGC 1316 (galaxy) 81
NGC 2023 (nebula) 159
NGC 2264 160
NGC 2440 (nebula) 124
NGC 2818 (nebula) 13
NGC 2841 (galaxy) 82
NGC 3132 (galaxy) 124
NGC 4261 (galaxy) 46
NGC 4650A (galaxy) 152
NGC 5189 (nebula) 124–125
NGC 5584 (galaxy) 75
NGC 5752 (galaxy) 145
NGC 5754 (galaxy) 145
NGC 6357 (nebula) 149
NGC 7049 (galaxy) 83
northern lights, *See* sun, aurora borealis
nuclear fusion 21, 46

O

Olympus Mons 60
Omega Centauri 31, 157
Omega Nebula 110
oort cloud 145
Orion Nebula X, 92–93
oxygen 110

P

Pan 68
Pandora 68
Pillars of Creation 95
Pistol Star 42, 44–45
planets 40, 52–72
plasma VII, 21–23, 25, 29, 43, 55, 140
Pleiades 134, 137
Pluto 35, 52, 64
Proctor Crater 61
Proxima Centauri 11, 31, 35, 142
Ptolemy 12

Q

quasars VII, 44–45

R

radiation 44, 55, 93, 103–104, 108, 110, 118, 123–124, 139–140, 143
radio waves 139–140
Red Rectangle *See* HD 44179
Retina Nebula 126–127
Rigel 38–40
Ring Nebula 126–127

S

S106 128
Sagittarius 110, 117
Saturn 40–41, 53, 64–69
SETI (Search for Extra-Terrestrial Intelligence) 156, 159
Shoemaker-Levy 9, 62–63
Sirius 38–40
Small Magellanic Cloud 111
SNR 0509-67.5 (supernova remnant) 49
solar system 28, 38, 52–53, 57, 60, 62–63, 69–71, 93, 96, 118, 121, 145, 153, 155
Sombrero Galaxy. *See* Messier 104 (galaxy)
Southern Ring Nebula. *See* NGC 3132 (galaxy)
stars VII, 11, 21, 31–51
   distance to 28, 31, 35
   dying stars 118–120, 123–124, 126
   energy of 21, 42, 44
   number of 12, 15

pulsars VII, 45–46, 162
Steady State Theory 143
Sun VII, 21–29
  aurora borealis 25, 27
  coronal mass ejection 24–25, 27, 43
  energy of 21, 42
  prominences 22–23, 28
  size of 28, 31, 35, 38–41
  solar flare 25, 28–29
  sunspots 23–25
supercluster 155
Supernova 1987A 49
supernovas VII, 45–47, 49–50, 73, 78, 151, 162
Swan Nebula. *See* Omega Nebula

T
Tadpole Galaxy 87
Tarantula Nebula 113
The Mice 85
thermodynamics 16
The Rose 88
Titan 68
Trifid Nebula 15, 116–117
Triton 71

U
Uranus 38, 40, 53, 69–71, 145

V
V838 Monocerotis 130
Valles Marineris 58, 60
Vela Nebula 163
Venus VII, 40, 53, 56–58, 70
Virgo Supercluster IX, 155
Voyager 1 153, 155
Voyager 2 69–71
VY Canis Majoris 38–41, 142

W
Whirlpool Cross 153
Whirlpool Galaxy 150, 152–153

X
X-rays 49, 139

Z
Zeta Ophiuchi 138